forever

forever

Why You Can't *Live* Without It

PAUL DAVID TRIPP

ZONDERVAN®

ZONDERVAN.com/
AUTHORTRACKER
follow your favorite authors

ZONDERVAN

Forever
Copyright © 2011 by Paul David Tripp

This title is also available as a Zondervan ebook. Visit www.zondervan.com/ebooks.

This title is also available in a Zondervan audio edition. Visit www.zondervan.fm.

Requests for information should be addressed to:
Zondervan, *Grand Rapids, Michigan 49530*

Library of Congress Cataloging-in-Publication Data

Tripp, Paul David, 1950-
    Forever : why you can't live without it / Paul David Tripp.
       p. cm.
    Includes bibliographical references.
    ISBN 978-0-310-32818-6 (softcover)
    1. Immortality—Christianity. 2. Future life—Christianity. 3. Eternity. I. Title.
BT921.3.T75 2011
236'.21—dc23   2011018819

Published in association with the literary agency of Ann Spangler & Company, 1420 Pontiac Road SE, Grand Rapids, MI 49506.

Cover design: *John Hamilton Design*
Cover photography: *GettyImages®*
Interior design: *Matthew Van Zomeren*

Printed in the United States of America

11 12 13 14 15 16 17 18 /DCI/ 20 19 18 17 16 15 14 13 12 11 10 9 8 7 6 5 4 3 2 1

To all the people who have helped me understand the depth of the beauty of the grace of Jesus. I could not do what God has called me to do without you.

CONTENTS

ACKNOWLEDGMENTS

To Malcolm Osborn and Steve and Gail Sarkisian, thank you for your love, support, and faithful friendship. I couldn't do what I'm doing without you. To Ann Spangler and Sandy Vander Zicht, thank you for making this book what it is. Finally, Luella, you are both my inspiration and dearest friend. Thank you for being willing to make the sacrifices that you have so that I could follow the Lord on the journey he's led me.

THE EVIDENCE
IS EVERYWHERE

Why is it so hard for us to be satisfied?

Why do so many of our marriages struggle over the long run?

Why do we have such a hard time getting along with family and friends?

Why do we carry around so much debt?

Why do we stand in front of full closets and say we have nothing to wear?

Why do we look into fully stocked refrigerators and say we have nothing to eat?

Why do so many of us consistently spend more than we earn?

Why do we struggle so much with envy?

Why does our culture tend to be overdrugged and oversexed?

Why do we spend so much on making sure that we are incessantly entertained?

Why do our trials paralyze us more than they should?

Why do people disappoint us so easily?

Why does life in the here and now never seem to deliver what we hoped it would deliver?

Why?

Where do you go, where do you look for answers to questions like this? What helps you to understand life? We all want to do it. We're all investigators trying to solve the mystery that is our own life. We all ask questions, and we all search for answers. At times, not knowing and not understanding doesn't bother us because we are locked in our busy schedules, distracted by the details of life or thankful that our life is comfortable at the moment. At other times, not knowing is painful and scary because we are facing something we can't ignore but are unable to make sense of.

Where do you look for meaning and purpose? What do you reach for to give you that inner rest and well-being that every one of us seeks? What unpacks and explains life for you? All of us want to think that what we believe is true. All of us want to think that we are living life the way it is meant to be lived and are prepared for what is to come. But the evidence is that many of us aren't. The evidence is all around us: *something is wrong.*

I saw this evidence again and again as I sat with clients in life-changing moments of disappointment, anger, confusion, and grief. I helped them tell their stories so I could interpret their stories from the unique perspective of the one story that could make sense of it all: God's story, unfolded in the pages of the Bible. I listened to the man who had lost his job and in so doing had lost himself, the woman dealing with marriage disappointment, or the person who was simply lost in the middle of his own story.

Again and again I sat there thinking, "What I need to do is give eternity back to this person." It became increasingly clear that many of the people I counseled were struggling because there was a critical element in their story that they either never knew or had completely forgotten. And it wasn't too long after reaching this conclusion that I began to admit to myself that I was more like the people I counseled than unlike them.

Like them, I often lived as an eternity amnesiac. I, too, often lived with the unrealistic expectations and functional hopelessness that always results when you tell yourself that this life you have right here, right now, is all there is. I was confronted with the fact that in very significant ways, at street level, we don't always live in a way consistent with what we confess to believe.

One of my reasons for writing this book was to tell the story of the many people whom God brought my way in dark passages of their lives. (Of course, I have altered the details of their lives to protect their identities.) I wanted to do more than tell their stories; I wanted to tell my story. But I wanted to do even more than that. I wanted to help you understand our stories and yours from the unique perspective of forever so you would begin to understand that the unshakable promise of the future grace of eternity does more than give you hope for the future. No, embedded in the promise of a future is the guarantee of grace for what you're facing right here, right now. You see, the God of eternity enters your story in the here and now, or he couldn't guarantee your future. And that makes all the difference in the world.

Perhaps you too have pockets of confusion. Maybe there are moments when you feel overwhelmed. Maybe you're near someone who has lost hope. Perhaps there's a place in your life where you are looking for a reason to continue. Keep reading and you will find people like you, but you'll find more. You'll find the most beautiful story ever told. It is the only story big enough to make sense out of our little stories, and it is the only story that guarantees the one thing you and I daily need: grace.

The book you are about to read is not written only out of my own experience or my parents' wisdom. It looks at life based on the wisdom of the Book of books, the Bible. The Bible is God's origin-to-destiny manual for living. There is no more reliable place to look to understand life, even at street level, than the Maker's book, the Bible.

God's Book is so rich and deep that you can pull on the thread of one theme and gain more practical, life-shaping wisdom than you ever would have imagined possible. So in this book I've taken one wisdom perspective from God's Word and looked at life from that perspective—the perspective of eternity.

The story of the Bible doesn't end with this world that we are all living in right now. What would seem like the last chapter, death, really isn't the last chapter in God's story. The Bible welcomes and requires you to face the inescapable reality of life after death. This present life is not all there is. There is a forever on the other side of this life. Eternity is not a mystical creation of overly spiritual people. Forever is a reality. It is the product of God's plan and design. And once you believe in forever and live with forever in view, not only will you understand things you have never understood before, but you will live in a radically different way than you did before.

So I invite you to step off the treadmill of your busy life and consider what life looks like when viewed through the lens of forever. What if this present life is not a destination but a preparation for a final destination? What if you and I have forever hardwired inside of us? What if this life really does have consequences in the next? What if human beings were created to live forever? What if you can't make sense out of life without eternity?

Then what?

Chapter One

WHO STOLE FOREVER?

No matter who you are, where you are, and how old you are, you long for a perfect world and struggle with the fact that the address where you live is anything but perfect. The young couple getting married have visions of the perfect marriage free from the struggles that they have seen others have. The pregnant mom dreams of giving birth to a perfect baby, easy to parent in every way. We imagine the perfect meal, the perfect job, the perfect vacation, the perfect house on the perfect street, the perfect friendship, and the perfect retirement. The list is endless. We're all dreamers because we all have forever wired inside us. It's hard for us to be content with the world that is, because all of us have an inclination to crave for what could be. We're not perfect, the people we live with are not perfect, and the world around us surely isn't perfect, yet the dream lives on in unrealistic expectations and dashed hopes. We are forever people; it is the way we were designed. We were created to live in a perfect world where death didn't exist and where life would give way to life on into eternity. So we hope much, dream much, imagine much, groan much, sorrow much, and cry much.

Every human being recognizes that this is not the way things were meant to be. Children aren't supposed to grow up and never know their biological parents. Husbands and wives were not meant to leave one another in the heat of acrimony, hurt, and selfishness. Boys and girls aren't supposed to live in the daily fear of the mockery of peers. Pleasurable experiences and substances aren't supposed to have the power to addict us. The world shouldn't be scarred by violence and war. Your skin color shouldn't be a reason for being rejected. Human beings were not meant to use other human beings for their own pleasure. Government was meant to protect people, not to use people to consolidate its own power. Human lives were not meant to be cut short by hunger, natural disaster, or disease. Innocent peoples' futures were not meant to be destroyed by political and financial scams. A person's capacity to hope was never intended to be kidnapped by false hope. Daughters were never meant to despise their mothers, or sons their fathers. Siblings were never meant to spend their developmental years in daily conflict with one another. The soil of earth was never designed to grow weeds better than it produces food and flowers. No person was meant to go to sleep with tears or wake up with anxiety or dread.

In some way we all get it. At some level we all understand. No, we may not have stopped to meditate on it, and we may not be able to articulate the sense that we carry around, but we all know this is not the way things were meant to be. So we imagine, we dream, we hope and pray. We kick the chair in frustration, hang up the phone in anger, or silently cry in hurt. We have forever inside us, and it creates a natural disappointment with the brokenness of the here and now. Let me show you what I mean.

we groan for more, for God

DREAMS OF A PERFECT WORLD

He looked out the window of his penthouse in Philadelphia onto the lush greenery of Rittenhouse Square, but he didn't notice it;

Josh was too deep in his thoughts. The last five years had been a row house to penthouse ride. The pharmaceutical company that hired him had exploded with growth, and Josh was a benefactor. He had always dreamed of this kind of success, and he had worked hard to get where he was. From his clothes to his car to his penthouse, Josh had acquired all the accoutrements of success. But what occupied his thoughts and what drove him crazy was one inescapable fact: he wasn't happy and he didn't feel fulfilled. Sure, he enjoyed the things that he was now able to afford, and when he was out with his friends, he could laugh with the best of them. The quiet moments were what got to him. What he felt just before he went to sleep or when he was in that "still lying in bed, but I've got to get up" fog was what he hated. He had worked hard for many years. He had delayed getting married. He had been willing to alienate friends and crush competitors to be able to experience what he thought would be the good life, and now that he had it, it just didn't mean what he thought it would mean.

No, Josh wasn't about to quit his job and sell the penthouse, but he was tired of having it all and feeling as though he didn't.

Sally couldn't believe it was still dark outside as she was yanking on her sweats one more predawn time. The alarm had somehow fit into that final early morning dream before the dream evaporated and she realized she was being summoned to face another day. She could already hear the kid noises down the hall reminding her that there wasn't much time between putting on her sweats and putting the kids on the bus. Her mind began to buzz through the breakfast menu, a mental assembly of lunches, and an assessment of what clothes were clean and ready for each child to wear. She walked down the hallway, and as she stretched and yawned, she wondered how she pulled it off day after day.

It seemed at times as if her life was living her rather than her living her life. Her husband's voice yanked her back to reality, announcing that he had an early meeting and was about to leave.

Sally yelled an "I love you" as she chased their son Jared down the hall, carrying the clothes he didn't really want to put on. She could probably make breakfast and lunches with her eyes closed, and it seemed that was exactly what she was doing this morning.

After the final kid was on the final bus, Sally sat slumped on the big leather couch in the family room with the requisite cup of Earl Grey tea, and she had trouble remembering the morning she had just been through. Had she been patient with the kids? Were they all dressed appropriately? Did they all eat breakfast? What in the world was in their lunches?

Often on these frenetic school mornings, Sally's head wasn't in her own life. She had begun to feel that most of the time she was elsewhere. It was not that she was unhappy or that she wanted out. Sally loved Jack, and she had always wanted children. The routine was what got to Sally. It felt like the proverbial roller coaster that never stops but goes and goes and always ends up at the same place. Is this what life was about—repetitive routines on an endless stream of similar days?

Sally didn't want to change anything, but as she got up to restore order to the kitchen, she told herself that she was not satisfied with what she was feeling.

Josh and Sally, two people who seem to be different from each other, are deep down very much the same. They share the same dream, and they are in the middle of the same struggle. Hardwired inside each of them is a desire for life to mean something, for it to be going somewhere. Hardwired inside of each of them is distaste for meaninglessness. Hardwired into the very cells of their personhood is a thing called eternity. Deep inside them is a cry for forever.

The curse of the old man at his inability to get his leg to do what it was meant to do is a cry for forever. The hurt inside the teenager who has been mocked by a peer is more than adolescent angst; it is a cry for forever. The whimper of the toddler who has had a toy wrenched from his hands by his older brother is more than a scream of protest; it is a cry for forever. The tears of a mom at the end of a talk with a lost and wayward son are more than tears of parental grief; they are the tears for forever. The anger of the man who has just been laid off by a boss who didn't seem to care is more than anger at a career injustice; it is a plea for forever. The sad silence around the casket of a dear one is more than the silence of the bereaved; it is a wordless longing for forever. The frustration of the erstwhile gardener that weeds grow faster than the flowers is more than a fight with the forces of nature; it is a wish that forever would come.

Forever is more than a hope and a dream. It is more than a theological formulation. It is more than a distant spiritual expectation. The Creator placed forever inside you. Longing for eternity doesn't mean you're spiritual; it simply means you are human. Life that never ends was the Maker's original plan.

Now, I'm not saying that we all live with a consciousness of forever or with an intentionality about life that is formed by a belief in forever. I'm not talking about forever as an essential piece of our theological paradigm. I'm not talking about how you are thinking about eternity or what you are doing about eternity. I'm talking about something God wired inside you when he made you. If you are a human being, you are a forever being. So much of your distress at what is, is really a hunger for what will be. It is just the way you were made. You may not have been aware of it, but this longing for paradise is an essential part of what makes you human and on a moment-by-moment personal quest. Yes, paradise has been hardwired inside all of us.

You may escape formal religion. You may avoid signing on to some theological system. You may question whether there is such a thing as life after death. You may think that the concept of a heaven and a hell should be left for naive, unscientific Christians. You may never call yourself a Presbyterian, Buddhist, Lutheran, Hindu, Mormon, Baptist, or Muslim, but you will also never successfully escape forever. It is inside you. It has been constructed inside you by your Maker. You and I didn't have a vote. We were hardwired for eternity. We were made to live forever. This is not first a matter of what we believe; it is first a matter of who we are. Eternity lives and longs inside us; there is simply no escaping it. This is why Josh and Sally struggle. This is why you and I struggle. Deep inside each of us is a cry for forever. It is every human's struggle this side of eternity. That is why the whole world groans. (If you have a Bible near, read Romans 8:18 – 27.)

SOMEONE STOLE SOMETHING, BUT WE DIDN'T NOTICE

If we understood this reality and lived as if it were true, much of our discontent would disappear. But it isn't that simple, because we don't believe in eternity anymore. Sure, if you poll average citizens in Western culture as to whether they believe in an afterlife, most respondents will tell you that they do. The problem is that eternity doesn't mean anything to most people. It's not formative in the way they live their everyday lives. As a culture, we believe in eternity the way we believe in God. Most people say they do, but you wouldn't know it from observing the way they live. Most people live in a constant state of *eternity amnesia*.

We have abandoned a self-conscious allegiance to the reality of eternity that structures the way we think about and approach the here and now. The functional philosophy of the modern person is simply devoid of eternity. Forever isn't a topic written about much in our newspapers and magazines. It isn't a topic of interest in our popular entertainment media. It isn't a serious topic of interest in the university or in the halls of government. The thought of forever simply isn't a thought many of us carry around anymore, at least not in a way that makes much difference. We're forever people who have lost sight of forever.

Is it odd to think of eternity as being a topic of interest in the university classroom? Yet this was once the case. The finest institutions of higher education in America—Harvard, Princeton, and Yale, for example—were all founded by people who held firmly to a biblical worldview that has eternity as its final hope. Yet today eternity is not a category that our culture takes seriously when we think of what life is all about. Consider, for a moment, the huge philosophical transition that has taken place in the way the average person thinks about life. We have gone from the words that Ben Franklin penned for his own epitaph:

> The Body
> Of
> Benjamin Franklin,
> Printer,
> (Like the cover of an old book,
> Its contents torn out,
> And stript of its lettering and gilding,)
> Lies here, food for worms.
> But the work shall not be lost,
> For it will, as he believed, appear once more,
> In a new and more elegant edition,
> Revised and corrected
> By
> The Author.[1]

To the bitter words of bestselling novelist Frank McCord: "I had to get rid of any idea of hell or any idea of the afterlife. That's what held me, kept me down. So now I just have nothing but contempt for the institution of the church."[2]

In our functional worldview, we have traveled from the eternity-driven lyrics of Julia Ward Howe's "Battle Hymn of the Republic"—

> Mine eyes have seen the glory of the coming of the Lord;
> He is trampling out the vintage where the grapes of wrath are
>   stored;
> He hath loosed the fateful lightning of His terrible swift sword;
> His truth is marching on.

Forever

Refrain:
Glory, glory, hallelujah!
Glory, glory, hallelujah!
Glory, glory, hallelujah!
Our God is marching on.

I have seen Him in the watch-fires of a hundred circling camps;
They have builded Him an altar in the evening dews and damps;
I can read His righteous sentence by the dim and flaring lamps;
His day is marching on.

I have read a fiery gospel writ in burnished rows of steel:
"As ye deal with my condemners, so with you my grace shall deal;
Let the Hero, born of woman, crush the serpent with His heel,
Since God is marching on."

He has sounded forth the trumpet that shall never call retreat;
He is sifting out the hearts of men before His judgment-seat;
Oh, be swift, my soul, to answer Him! be jubilant, my feet!
Our God is marching on.

In the beauty of the lilies Christ was born across the sea,
With a glory in His bosom that transfigures you and me;
As He died to make men holy, let us die to make men free,
While God is marching on.

He is coming like the glory of the morning on the wave;
He is wisdom to the mighty, He is succour to the brave,
So the world shall be His footstool, and the soul of Time His slave,
Our God is marching on.

—to the content of popular entertainment and social media that has little sense of reality beyond an obsession with the pleasures and comforts of the here and now. Consider the words from a blog post by University of Minnesota professor Paul Zachary "PZ" Myers: "That is the godless view of death. It's an end, not a transition. It deserves all the sorrow the living bring to it, and the absurd attempts of believers to soften it with lies are a contemptible disservice to the life that is over."[3]

This change in worldview does beg the question, "Who stole forever?" No, there is no bunker where a group of nefarious philosophers are plotting the philosophical demise of Western culture. But the functional worldview of Western culture denies a belief in the hereafter.

The shift has been subtle but nonetheless seismic in its impact. This life-altering change didn't begin a few years ago. It has been percolating for generations. The movement away from a biblical view of life coupled with the materialism of our modern scientific culture has affected the way we think about who we are and what is important.

The larceny of forever shapes our lives more than we realize. Eternity amnesia grips us all, making it hard, if not impossible, for us to imagine living forever. We find it hard to believe in anything that contradicts the "here and now is all you get" perspective that rules the day. So we have functionally discarded the once widely held belief in an afterlife, a reality we cannot embrace without it influencing the way we live. Without forever in the center of our thinking, our picture of life is like a jigsaw puzzle missing a central piece. You will simply not have an accurate view of the picture without the piece of the puzzle entitled "forever."

This void has had an enormous impact on how we think about ourselves and the struggles we daily face. When it comes to the university classroom, the public square, and popular media, the concept of eternity is fundamentally absent. You will never hear Katie Couric close her nightly news broadcast by saying, "I know things often look bleak and chaotic, but remember that this is not all there is. We are all heading for eternity, where all that is broken will be finally and forever fixed. This is Katie Couric, *CBS News*. Good night." Children watching morning TV have been robbed of forever. Junior high kids studying history will not be taught how to examine history through the lens of forever. University students in a psychology class will not be assigned an essay on the impact of eternity on a human being's emotions and behavior. Most businesspeople investing money don't have eternity in their minds, let alone in the way they think about their portfolio.

Forever

Most couples embracing one another at the altar don't get the importance of also embracing the sure and coming reality of forever. The young mother looking at her newborn doesn't think that forever is hardwired inside her child. So someone has entered the house of Western culture and stolen a precious family heirloom, but most of us don't know a robbery has taken place. We go on living as if nothing has happened, but it has, and in powerful and practical ways it affects us all.

We get up in the morning and do the kinds of things people have done for generations. We buy and sell, plant and harvest. We relate, commit, laugh, love, and fight. We get married and we make families. We work hard, create things, and reengineer our surroundings. Some of us build cities, and others of us thank God for the suburbs. We think, we analyze, and we critique. We try to learn from our mistakes, and we attempt to educate and prepare the next generation. We spend lots of our time eating and sleeping. We hate to be lonely, and we do our best to avoid pain. We search for meaning and purpose, and all of us long for an inner sense of well-being. We have eternity amnesia, and consequently our lives are much more difficult than they need to be.

Here is a quick overview of the consequences of eternity amnesia on our lives.

1. *Living with unrealistic expectations.* Why are our expectations less than realistic? Because in our eternity amnesia we are asking this present world to be what it simply never will be. We want the here and now to behave as if it is our final destination, when actually all that we are experiencing in the here and now prepares us for the destination that is to come.

2. *Focusing too much on self.* Human beings were created to live big-picture, long-view lives. We were made to live with something bigger in view than this present moment's comfort, pleasure, and happiness. Eternity confronts us with the fact that we are not in charge, that

we do not live in the center of the universe, and that life moves by the will and purpose of Another. The instantaneous, self-serving, me obsession of our culture never results in inner peace and contentment. Eternity confronts me with the realities that transcend my momentary wants, feelings, and needs.

3. *Asking too much of people.* When we fail to live with forever in view, we unwittingly and consistently ask the people around us to provide the paradise for which our hearts crave. The people around us do not have the ability to give us, in the here and now, that constant inner peace and satisfaction that we can only ever experience in eternity. Asking others to give us what they cannot give ends in disappointment, frustration, conflict, and division.

4. *Being controlling or fearful.* Why do we tend to swing from fear to control and back again? Because, in our eternity amnesia, we feel as if somehow, someway, life is passing us by. Those unfilled longings, which none of us escape, do not so much announce to us that this world has failed us, but rather they alert us to the fact that we were designed for another world. Peace in this world is found only when we live with the coming world in view.

5. *Questioning the goodness of God.* If we don't understand God's agenda, we will tend to end up questioning his character. Unless we live in the knowledge that God's promises only reach their fulfillment in the world that is to come, we will feel as if we have been hit with the cosmic bait and switch in the world we now live in. We get a taste of God's good gifts in the here and now to keep us hungering for the full meal that is waiting for us in eternity.

6. *Living more disappointed than thankful.* Unrealistic expectations will always lead to disappointment. Many of us are disappointed, not because God has failed us, or we have suffered much, or the people around us have

been particularly difficult to live with, but because we approach life hoping that it will deliver to us things that we can only experience in eternity. Our disappointment reveals more about our own eternity amnesia than it does about the world around us.

7. *Lacking motivation and hope.* All of these consequences weaken our motivation and our hope. The fact that this world is not an endless cycle of dashed hopes and fading dreams but by God's plan is marching toward a moment when all that is broken will be restored can fill you with a reason to get up in the morning and press on. Yes, life is hard and you will face things you never imagined you would face, but this world is not all there is. You are not living in the final chapter of the story. What is broken will be fixed, what has been bent will be straightened, and what has decayed will be restored. Eternity really does give you a reason to continue, even when nothing right now seems as if it is working. Eternity challenges my feelings of futility by reminding me that what I am experiencing right now is not permanent.

8. *Living as if life doesn't have consequences.* Eternity forces me to face the fact that life does have consequences. We can believe whatever we want to believe and live however we want to live, but we will face the consequences of poor choices. There is life after death, and I could argue that eternity *is* the ultimate consequence. A day of reckoning is coming that no human being will escape, and realizing that reality infuses today with a moral seriousness that you will find no other way.

WELCOME TO YOUR SCHIZOPHRENIA

We are forever people who have quit believing in forever. We live in the middle of a massive contradiction. No, I'm not talking about the functional demise of organized religion. I'm encouraging you to think about something fundamentally profounder than that. I am getting you to think about the intersection between who you are by design and how you live every day. Perhaps I should state it more forcefully. The *forever-ism* that is hardwired inside you collides with the *now-ism* that is everywhere around you, resulting in a lot of carnage.

What we all internally long for in some way collides with what we end up living for every day. What we were hardwired to be collides with how we live. What was designed to propel everything we do collides with what motivates us. What our minds were designed to grasp and hold on to collides with what our senses tell us is real. In our heart of hearts, in myriad situations of life, the future wars with the present. It is one of the abiding contradictions of modern human life yet was never meant to be this way. Now was designed to be an introduction to hereafter, and hereafter was designed to be the living hope of now. But the schizophrenia is all around us.

Most of us will live in a state of happy delusion, failing to grasp the beauty we have missed as we live in a way we were never meant to live. Consider these words of C. S. Lewis.

> Most of us find it very difficult to want "Heaven" at all — except in so far as "Heaven" means meeting again our friends who have died. One reason for this difficulty is that we have not been trained: our whole education tends to fix our minds on this world. Another reason is that when the real want for Heaven is present in us, we do not recognize it. Most people, if they really learned to look into their own hearts, would know that they do want, and want acutely, something that cannot be had in this world. There are all sorts of things in this world that offer to give it to you, but they never quite keep their promise.[4]

Life, real life as it was designed to be, simply cannot work without eternity. It is the nature of design. You will never see your neighbor drive his speedboat out of his garage and down the street. His boat is an amazing creation, but it was not designed to travel over macadam. You will never see a fish lounging in a tree. Everything around us only works, is used, or lives according to its design.

You were made for forever. That is your inescapable identity. Life only works as it was meant to work when you live with forever in view. Could it be that you have been like a bird underwater, trying your best to find life in the here and now while forgetting forever? There really is a better way.

These words by C. S. Lewis say it all: "If I find in myself a desire which no experience in this world can satisfy, the most probable explanation is that I was made for another world."[5]

Chapter Two

THE PACK-IT-ALL-IN MENTALITY

Jack wasn't a philosophical guy; he didn't step back and examine why he did the things he did. But he did think about one thing: his debt. It had simply gotten out of control. He had burned through his savings and liquidated a couple of retirement accounts, and he still wasn't keeping up with his creditors' demands. His problem wasn't the economy. No, he had a great job that paid him well. His problem was that his cravings were bigger than his paycheck.

Raised in a poor family, Jack determined early that he was going to be financially successful and give his family all the things that he had had to live without. He worked himself up the ladder and gave his family things he wouldn't have dreamed of as a child. The house Jack and his wife, Jennifer, decided on was bigger than what they needed, and the pool out back was just too cool to resist. Turning the family room into a full-blown game room was expensive, but it kept the kids from getting bored. The vacation home at the shore was the icing on the cake — a place where memories would be made. Jack's "buy the best and then you have no regrets" philosophy fueled their debt. Sure, the gourmet kitchen with its top-of-the-line appliances was used way too little, but those dinners out as a family surely did break up the week. Yes, the debt load was a bit scary, but no one was taking drugs or committing adultery; and anyway, didn't God create these things for us to enjoy?

But hiding the debt from Jennifer was getting harder and harder to do, and Jack knew that if his wife found out, she would lose it. Jack had coped by shuffling money from account to account, but there wasn't much left to shuffle. His stomach would tighten as Jen left for the grocery store. He hoped and prayed her ATM card would not be rejected. Jen didn't know how often he waited to mail checks that she gave him because he needed to get funds into the account before they cleared.

As he lay in bed waiting for sleep to take him away from his financial woes, Jack beat himself up for being such a poor money manager. He rehearsed old financial decisions again and again, looking for the moment when things began to go bad, but all it got him was less sleep and more anxiety. On the way to work, Jack rehearsed the conversation he needed to have with Jennifer, but he never had it. Nothing was left in their home equity line, and he had no more friends he could tap for help. Jack couldn't figure out how he had made such a mess of things, and he wasn't creative enough to think of a way to turn it all around. What he didn't understand was that his problem was much deeper than a series of poor money decisions.

David and Beth were as excited as they had ever been. They were on their way to the airport for a culinary vacation around Europe. Paris, Madrid, Venice, and Berlin—they couldn't believe it. They were foodies—no doubt about it. They knew they ate out too much, and they had to face the fact that both of them had gained weight since they had married. But they lived in a big city populated by celebrity chefs who never seemed to stop opening cool new restaurants. Beth loved the gourmet kitchen they had designed and built together. It looked like a Food Network studio, and that's just what she had in mind. The fact that the kitchen redo had cost about a quarter of what they had paid for the house didn't seem to faze David and Beth. Beth was occasionally guilty that she didn't use the kitchen as much as she thought she would because they so frequently went out to eat. Maybe the wine cellar was a bit over the top, but it seemed to go with the kitchen, and they couldn't resist.

While reading *Bon Appétit* magazine, Beth discovered the culinary vacation. Sure, they were financially strapped, with the loan for the kitchen and all the implements they had charged to stock it properly, but this seemed too good to resist. When she showed the ad to David, he was immediately hooked and began finagling ways to finance it. The new credit card, with 0 percent interest for three months, made it possible. David didn't want to think about bills right now; he was about to hit some of Europe's finest culinary destinations, and he wanted to savor what was to come. His boss was not excited about him taking extra vacation time, but David promised to work overtime when he got home to make up for the time off.

As they sat at the gate at the airport, Beth found it hard to believe they were about to do it. Not only would they eat as they never had before at places unlike any they had ever been, but they would also be hosted along the way by celebrity chefs! So much for her newly begun diet. Beth was not about to be bothered by calorie or cholesterol counts for the next two weeks. She was not about to waste the $3,500 apiece that she and David had invested in this trip by being anything less than a full participant. David and Beth loved the "good life," and as they boarded the jet, they knew it was about to get a whole lot better — at least for the next two weeks. They would deal with their bills and waistlines later.

RIGHT HERE, RIGHT NOW

Jack, David, and Beth all have eternity amnesia. They are living as if this life is all there is. If this is all the life we have, then the name of the game is this: experience, possess, and accomplish everything we can, right here, right now, because this is all there is. The old beer commercial captured it powerfully: "You only go around once in life, so you've got to grab for all the gusto you can." If you're not moving toward a glory so glorious that it will overwhelm the pain of anything you suffer, then this is all the glory you will ever get. Don't sit on the sidelines. Don't find reasons to say no. Pack everything you can into this moment, because this moment is all you are ever going to have.

Jack, David, and Beth are not alone. Hundreds and thousands of the people around them are doing the same thing—loading all their hopes and dreams into this present moment. Eternity amnesia makes present pleasures more magnetic and seductive and present difficulties more painful and disappointing, so we obsessively work to experience the good thing and, in anxiety, do everything we can to avoid the bad thing. This way of living makes us crazy in ways we may not be able to recognize.

Think of Jack. His life plan can't work, because a person simply cannot continue to spend more than he makes. And he cannot be successful for long at robbing one account to finance the needs of another. But Jack's problem isn't really financial. He has a forever problem. He is so driven to fix his own story right here and right now that he has gotten himself into a mess that he probably won't be able to get himself out of. At street level, Jack is a man without eternity. All he knows to do is dig deeper and work harder and hope that the "good life" that he has cobbled together won't suddenly crumble at his feet.

Jack thinks that he is offering his family the "good life," but it isn't that good after all. As a husband, he is tense and uptight, ready to argue over every penny Jen wants to spend. As a dad, he is seldom at home because he is working constantly to stay ahead of financial doom. And when he is home, he is not the relaxed relational dad that every child needs. Jack's children will remember the big house and the vacation home, but they will also remember Dad's absence and distance.

Consider how different things would be if Jack understood what eternity teaches us about the here and now. Imagine if he understood that the deepest, most satisfying joys are not to be found in the possessions and experiences of this brief here-and-now moment. Imagine if that freed Jack to be content with a smaller home, a summer rental at the beach, and fewer toys for him and the children. Imagine if Jack remembered every day that the God who was moving him toward eternity would give him everything he needed along the way. Then Jack wouldn't need to work as much, he wouldn't need to worry as much, and he could spend more time doing the most important work assigned to him this side of forever: lovingly serving his wife and joyfully parenting his children.

David and Beth are also committed to a lifestyle that will not work. They are modern-day epicureans on a pathway to disappointment. Maybe the deal breaker will be bills that they are unable to pay or a health issue that alters life as they know it, but the pleasure-at-any-cost paradigm won't work in the long run. They have placed all of their joy in the basket of physical, material experiences in the here and now. They are so convinced that the good life is a life of present, physical pleasure that they have forced themselves not to look at the real cost (personal, relational, and financial) of this kind of lifestyle. While celebrating here and now, they have become skilled at denying the inescapable realities of here and now. They are engaging in a "smile and deny" way of living that is much emptier and more dangerous than they understand.

Beth and David don't have a food problem. They have an eternity problem that results in food being in a place it should not be. Cutting the foodie aspect out of their lifestyle would not solve their problem, because their pack-it-all-into-the-here-and-now quest would just migrate to another arena, and they would be as driven and in danger as they are in the area of food.

Jack, David, and Beth each need to be rescued from a view of life that has no movement toward eternity. They need to be rescued from the here-and-now drivenness of their own functional present-ism. Jack, David, and Beth need forever to be given back to them. It is the only way real change will take place in the way they live.

DESTINATION VERSUS PREPARATION

Many of us treat here and now as a destination. Whatever our confessional theology says about eternity, at the functional level we live as if this is all there is. We live with a *destination mentality* instead of a *preparation mentality*. This present world with all of its joys and sorrows is not our final address. When we treat it as if it is, we try to get from this world what we can only experience in the next. We try to pack into our present life all the pleasure, happiness, and excitement we can. We do this because what comes with the thought that this life is all there is, is an inescapable fear that somehow life will pass us by. Here is what a destination mentality fails to understand: our complete, present, personal happiness is not what God is working on in the here and now. Why? Because the plan of his grace is to deliver us out of this world to one that is much, much better. Whether we live with eternity in view or not, there is one thing we all need to understand: God always responds to us with eternity in view.

You see, God has designed that this would not be the final destination for his children. He knows that this is a terribly broken world that, in its present state, does not function the way that he intended. This world is not a safe place to look to for a sense of well-being. For that, we need to live with a preparation mentality, approaching each day knowing that this world is not intended to be our final destination, and that God is preparing another world for us. Living with a preparation mentality also means living with the knowledge that God is using the disappointments and difficulties of this world to prepare us for the next. God uses the pressures of the present to craft us into the kind of individuals with whom he would choose to spend eternity.

Living in this present world is designed by God to produce three things in me—*longing, readiness, and hope.* Rather than deepening my drive to have it all now, the disappointments of this present world are intended to make me long for the next. God also knows that we are not ready for the world that is to come. There are ways in which we still are too impressed with our own wisdom, strength, and righteousness. We still struggle to love the Creator more than the creation. We still want to have our own way and write our own rules. So there are important character changes that grace needs to work in us to make us ready for our final destination. And God is using this present moment to produce in us sturdy hope. As by his grace we experience tastes of what is to come, we don't panic in the face of difficulty and disappointment, because we know that God is moving us toward a place where the suffering of this present moment will be no more.

When we ask now to give us what only eternity can, we end up driven, frustrated, discouraged, and ultimately hopeless. We begin with unrealistic expectations and end feeling as though life has passed us by. We try to exercise more control than any person ever has over their circumstances and relationships in order to ensure that we get what we have set our hopes on. But we are not sovereign, and we soon realize it. Because we fall into thinking of this life as our final destination, we place more hope in our situations, relationships, and locations than they are able to deliver. We ask people, places, and things to satisfy our souls and redeem our pasts, but they can't. We require a broken world that is not functioning as God intended to make us happy, but it never can and never will. We place way too many expectations on the people in our lives, and they never reach our standards, and we tend to get hurt or angry when they don't. We reduce all of life to a personal comfort and pleasure delivery system, but life never operates the way we wish. Because we live as if this is all there is, we are perennially demanding and disappointed, thinking that we have been dealt a particularly difficult hand. We envy the people around us who appear to have what we don't, and we find it hard to celebrate the successes of others. With the assumption that this is our final destination, we constantly want more and better. We're never able to say, "I have enough." We possess too much, eat too much, spend too much, dream too much, demand too much, complain too much, expect too much, keep score too much, ask too much—and we are disappointed too much. You see, we don't need a better now; no, we need forever to reshape our here and now.

One of the good things the Bible keeps in front of us is that this is not all there is. The world and everything in it is marching toward eternity, and when we understand that, everything changes. You know you don't actually just go around once, so you don't expend all of your life energies trying to do with gusto all you can now. You know you won't experience it all in the here and now. You understand that this life is but a brief preparation for the forever that is to come and that the messiness and hardship of the here and now are not an interruption of the plan, but a part of the plan. The one who is in charge has chosen to keep you in a world that is less than perfect, not because he has forgotten you and what you need, but precisely because he loves you and is delivering to you exactly what you need.

As Jack, David, and Beth discovered, the pack-it-all-in mentality simply doesn't deliver. The frenetic pace of the "good life" doesn't result in the lasting peace, joy, and rest that they are seeking—for them or for the people around them. No, the legacy of destination living is drivenness, dissatisfaction, and disappointment. Sure there are temporary highs, but they are short-lived and work only to keep you driving toward the next bite of the "good life."

Peace is found only in knowing that this world is meant to prepare us for the next and that the temporary pleasures and pains of this world are not our final address. When we live knowing that the God of grace will lift us out of this broken world and is now readying us for the world to come, we can face difficulty without wanting to give up and experience pleasure without becoming addicted to it. We live with hope in our heart, eyes to the future, and hands holding this present world loosely.

Everything in this world is meant to be a preparation for the next. That means that your marriage isn't a destination; it is a preparation. Your job isn't a destination; it is a preparation. Your friendships and family aren't destinations; they are a preparation. The sight and sound, touch and taste experiences of this present world aren't a destination; they are a preparation for a final destination. No, it isn't wrong to celebrate marital sex or a beautiful bouquet, or a silky chocolate pie, or a wonderful painting, or a death-defying roller coaster. It is right to stop and smell the roses along the way — as long as you don't treat those roses as a final destination.

We're fat, disappointed, driven, in debt, and addicted because we treat this here-and-now moment as if it were all we have. We have acted as though it is a destination, when all that is going on now is somehow, someway a preparation for the final destination that is to come.

LONGING FOR HOME

One of the ways Scripture talks about the impermanence of the here and now is to say that we are dwelling in tents (2 Corinthians 5:1–5). This word picture is of pilgrims traveling toward their final destination, who set up their portable dwelling places along the way. Your tent reminds you that you are not at your destination yet. It announces to you that you are not yet home.

Most of us have no pilgrim experience, so perhaps the closest thing in our experience to the journey of a pilgrim is rustic camping. I am persuaded that the whole purpose of camping is to make a person long for home! On that first day in the woods, putting up the tent is exciting, but three days later your tent has unpleasant odors you can't explain. You love the taste of food cooked over an open flame (that's ash!), but three days later you are tired of foraging for wood and irritated by how fast it burns. You were excited at the prospect of catching your dinner from the stream running past your campsite, which is reported to be teeming with trout, but all you have snagged are the roots on the bottom.

You're now four days in and your back hurts, there seems to be no more felled wood to forage, and you're tired of keeping the fire going anyway. You look into what was once an ice- and food-filled cooler to see the family-sized steak you have reserved floating gray and oozing in a pool of blood-stained water. Suddenly you begin to think fondly of home. You think of your soft and inviting mattress, the stove in your kitchen where you just twist a knob and get flame, the red New York strips you left in the freezer, and the house that you are pleased to call your home. You stand there hoping that someone will break the silence and say, "Why don't we go home?" Your four days in the wilderness have accomplished their mission. They have prepared you to appreciate home!

But generally in America we treat camping as a destination rather than a temporary location. We camp in sixty-foot motor homes that have a kitchen like Emeril Legasse's, a forty-two-inch flat screen, air conditioning, and indoor plumbing. We work to make the campsite more comfortable than home! No wonder we don't care if we ever return. No wonder we want life to be one endless vacation. No wonder we want to pack it all in.

But the pack-it-all-in mentality is not only bad for the people around us who will never be able to measure up; it is debilitating to us as well. It ignores the fact that we are broken and our world is broken and that both are in need of redemption. And it misses the hope that someday what is wrong will be righted and what is broken will be fixed. Our world isn't a very good amusement park. No, it is a broken place groaning for redemption. Here is meant to make us long for forever. Here is meant to prepare us for eternity. Now is not about wishing for personal sovereignty so that we get our dream. Now is about crying out for a Savior, because like our world, you and I have something broken inside us and desperately need to be redeemed. There is more to come, and when we realize that there is, we will stop living as if this is our final destination.

Chapter Three

THE BAD
NEWS YOU
CAN'T ESCAPE

It's the one thing we all agree on, the one area where there is no human debate whatsoever. It's the one time in life when we all experience the same thing and act in similar ways. It's the one moment in life when everyone's thoughts, emotions, desires, words, and actions are predictable. We hate the thought of it, and we dread that it's coming and we can't do a thing about it. It's mysterious, frightening, discouraging, paralyzing, and sad. We hope we can escape it for a long time, and most of us wish it on no one. When it is near us, we don't know what to say and are unsure how to act. We feel helpless. The pain crushes us at the moment and often lingers in our heart for years. It is the ultimate interruption, the unwanted intruder. No one who is alive will escape it. *Death*.

Today someone is on a vigil, watching the vitality of life slowly seep away from a loved one. Somewhere someone will get that horrible call that someone near and dear to him has suddenly died. Somewhere today someone will be told she doesn't have long to live. Somewhere, with deep breaths and heart racing, someone will breathe a sigh of relief because he has escaped death for the moment. Somewhere today someone will be rehearsing her words, trying to figure out how to tell someone that a person near him has died. Somewhere today someone will cry herself to sleep because someone she loved has died.

Death is never easy. It's impossible to plan for it. It's hard to predict how you will react when death enters your door. Death never seems right. How is it that something this universal can seem so unnatural?

I vividly remember my dad slipping in and out of a coma. Alert or comatose, he was incapable of any meaningful personal connection of any kind. I knew death was around the corner. I sat there silent and sad, but inside I was screaming. So much unfinished business. So much that needed to be said that would never be said. So many wounds that would be left open, events that still needed to be unpacked. I wanted to hear his voice one more time. I wanted him to be tender, to be my dad one more time. I wanted him to get up and hug me. I wanted to know that we would have tomorrow. I wanted him to be alive. People say that death is normal, but this moment seemed anything but normal. I've never felt more unprepared or more ill at ease. I've never wanted something to end more than that horrible few hours. I've never felt more helpless. As I watched my dad's life slip away, I couldn't help thinking again and again, *This is not the way it's supposed to be!*

NOT PART OF THE ORIGINAL PLAN

Death feels so fundamentally unnatural because it *is* unnatural. Maybe you're thinking, "Paul, what are you talking about? Everything dies sooner or later." Yes, death is the inescapable end to all things in the here and now, but there is something that you have to understand: death was not part of the original plan. Death is the disastrous result of a devastating decision. Life forever was the plan. Death was not in view.

Forever

It's hard to imagine a world without death as a central, inescapable reality. After all, flowers die. The fruit on the kitchen counter doesn't stay fresh. New cars start to decay before we even drive off the lot. Our house doesn't remain new, and the dog is showing signs of age. So it's hard to imagine life without death. But it's important to grasp that this was not the way it was meant to be. You see, the only way to understand what is to come is to understand what was. The only way to understand how unnatural death in the here and now is, in a way that makes you hunger for what is to come, is to understand the world that once was. That world simply did not have death as an inevitable reality.

God created Adam and Eve to be forever beings. He created them to live in worshipful communion with him and mutual love for one another forever. He placed them in a lush garden where life was to give way to life on into eternity. There was no sickness. There was no murder. There were no lifestyle or environmental diseases. There was no suffering or decay. No one dreaded the end that was sure to come, because there was no end coming. Life thrived and reigned. What was basic and natural to the universe that God created was life: life unhindered, life uninterrupted, and life unending. The world burst with life on every side. There was a danger of death, but the reality and experience of death did not exist. What existed was life in the deepest, fullest, most expansive sense of what that means. It was a perfect world created by a perfect God and inhabited by a perfect man and woman made by God. Adam and Eve didn't have many limits. Their calling was simple and rules few. Stay inside God's boundaries and they would experience life uninterrupted. God said one of thousands of trees in that garden of delights was off limits. "Stay away from it. Do not touch it. Do not eat from it or you will die."

Adam and Eve were not needy and hungry. The perfect world perfectly supplied all they needed. They had few boundaries. But despite the freedom God gave them, they were not satisfied with their place or God's rules. They could not resist what had

42

been clearly forbidden. They listened to horrible and deceptive counsel.

Adam and Eve made a tragic choice. They decided to deny who they were and how they were designed to live. For one tragic moment, they quit living with life-forever-with-God in view. For one horrible moment, they experienced eternity amnesia and did what many of us do every day: live like this here and now is all there is. In the shrunken vision of momentary pleasure, they lost sight of eternity and did what was unthinkable: they treasured what was on the other side of God's boundaries more than they did the beauty of life forever with God. In that moment, they were too busy trying to *be* God to be motivated by forever *with* God.

For the temporary tastiness of succulent fruit and the delusional dream of independence from God, they chose death over life. In this moment of temptation, they seemed to have quit thinking, hearing, and seeing. In the truest and most comprehensive sense of what it means, Adam and Eve lost their senses. Hardwired for forever, they turned their backs on forever and decided to shrink their existence to a dream no bigger than "right here, right now." It was a stunning moment of rebellion against a kind and loving Creator, an astonishing rejection of his gift of life forever. But it was also a fundamental denial of their humanity. They were not created to live for themselves, but for God. And they had not been designed to die, but to live forever. The very thing that was not part of the original plan—death—now infected the earth. Death is now the inescapable consequence of the rebellion of people against the one who created them and placed them in a wonderful environment of perfection, life, and beauty.

So between us and forever lives this nasty thing called death. We think of death as normal, but our reactions to death give evidence that it is anything but normal. That is why we fight so hard to avoid death and grieve when it comes. That is why death's finality throws us for a loop and makes us wonder if we will ever recover. That is why we visit grave sites years after a person has died. That is why in the face of death we euphemistically say the person is "no longer with us," "has passed away," or "has gone home." We mean to cushion the blow of the horrible, disruptive reality we were never meant to experience because it was not part of the wise Creator's original plan. Since we have forever wired into our hearts, death is an inconceivable, dark reality. It is the ultimate, universal dread of humanity.

Humanity has created the technology to conquer many things. Diseases that once inflicted humanity have disappeared. We have been able to defeat social, economic, and cultural problems. But we have not defeated death. It looms large and powerful in front of us. That wilted bouquet, that stale slice of bread, the milk that has soured in the refrigerator, and the firewood that was once a tree out back all remind us that we live in a place where death is literally all around us. We cannot run and we cannot hide and we have no ability to defeat it. Death lives at our address, and there is no escaping.

But the death that reared its ugly head in that garden so long ago wasn't just physical death. Spiritual death entered the world too, separating us from the one thing that was meant to define and motivate every human being: God. Adam and Eve were created as spiritual beings whose spirits were alive to God. They were never created to be self-actualizing, self-directed, self-focused, autonomous beings. Adam and Eve were meant to get their deepest, life-shaping meaning vertically, in connection to God. Loving, worshipful submission to him was to be at the center of their lives. God-awareness and God-worship formed all that they thought, desired, and did. As designed, they found joy in communion with God. They were happy to obey. They found delight in loving God. They wanted to worship him. They got up every day and lived for God's glory. God was their greatest pleasure. They found their deepest source of personal satisfaction in him. Everything they thought and desired was rooted in worship of God. Everything they said and every action they took was connected to his glory.

They were now living in a community with God that was designed to last forever. But in an act of outrageous personal aggrandizement, Adam and Eve not only brought physical death into this world, but an even more horrible form of death, spiritual death.

As a result, all human beings are born spiritually dead. The spiritually dead do not seek or understand God. They don't offer him the worship that is his due or stay inside of his boundaries. They don't look to him for their satisfaction and peace. They don't prize his kingdom or seek his wisdom. In the most practical sense of what spiritual death means, they no longer recognize God's existence. Sin separates them from God, and there is nothing they can do in their own strength to bridge this horrible gap.

What do spiritually dead people do? They put themselves in the middle of their universe and look to things to give them what only God can give. They live for physical pleasure, not spiritual communion. They become obsessed with their own little kingdoms instead of with God's. They deny their dependency. They act as if they are autonomous and self-sufficient. They write their own laws and live to fulfill their own dreams. They live with the pleasures of this present, physical world as their highest hope and dream. Incessant pleasure researchers and accountants, they again and again ask, "Where are the best pleasures to be found?" and "Who around me has more pleasure than I do?"

But none of it works like they wish it would work, because they were not made to live this way. What looks like life really isn't life; it is death, the most devastating form of death, spiritual death. It is a life lived in separation from the satisfying pleasures of knowing God and living in communion with God forever. We see this in the screams of crib-bound infants who want their own way. We see it in the fights of siblings who hate having to share. We see it in the angst of the young woman who doesn't like the shape of her nose. We see it in the rebellion of the teenager who wants to write his own rules. We see it in the argument of the self-centered husband and wife. We see it in the bitterness of the middle-aged man who never realized his dream. We all forget God, insert ourselves in the middle of our world, and make life all about us.

WHEN GOD IS LEFT OUT

Maybe you're thinking, "Wow, Paul, that's awfully strong language." Well, think about what is left if God is out of the picture. Consider the words of Asaph in Psalm 73:

> Surely God is good to Israel,
>> to those who are pure in heart.
>
> But as for me, my feet had almost slipped;
>> I had nearly lost my foothold.
> For I envied the arrogant
>> when I saw the prosperity of the wicked.
>
> They have no struggles;
>> their bodies are healthy and strong.
> They are free from common human burdens;
>> they are not plagued by human ills.
> Therefore pride is their necklace;
>> they clothe themselves with violence.
> From their callous hearts comes iniquity;
>> their evil imaginations have no limits.
> They scoff, and speak with malice;
>> with arrogance they threaten oppression.
> Their mouths lay claim to heaven,
>> and their tongues take possession of the earth.
> Therefore their people turn to them
>> and drink up waters in abundance.
> They say, "How would God know?
>> Does the Most High know anything?"
>
> This is what the wicked are like —
>> always free of care, they go on amassing wealth.
>
> 13 Surely in vain I have kept my heart pure
>> and have washed my hands in innocence.
> All day long I have been afflicted,
>> and every morning brings new punishments.

If I had spoken out like that,
   I would have betrayed your children.
When I tried to understand all this,
   it troubled me deeply
till I entered the sanctuary of God;
   then I understood their final destiny.

[18] Surely you place them on slippery ground;
   you cast them down to ruin.
[19] How suddenly are they destroyed,
   completely swept away by terrors!
[20] They are like a dream when one awakes;
   when you arise, Lord,
   you will despise them as fantasies.

[21] When my heart was grieved
   and my spirit embittered,
[22] I was senseless and ignorant;
   I was a brute beast before you.

Yet I am always with you;
   you hold me by my right hand.
You guide me with your counsel,
   and afterward you will take me into glory.
Whom have I in heaven but you?
   And earth has nothing I desire besides you.
My flesh and my heart may fail,
   but God is the strength of my heart
   and my portion forever.

Those who are far from you will perish;
   you destroy all who are unfaithful to you.
But as for me, it is good to be near God.
   I have made the Sovereign LORD my refuge;
   I will tell of all your deeds.

Can you relate to Asaph's struggle? Asaph was eaten up with envy at the pleasure of the people around him, and to make it worse, these were bad people who didn't deserve it! He concluded that he had tried to be a good guy for nothing (v. 13). He was living for here-and-now pleasure, keeping a watchful eye on others and the size of their pleasure piles. Doing so caused him to be more envious, and in his envy, more dissatisfied, and in his dissatisfaction, angrier.

Verses 21 and 22 picture the silent struggle of heart that many of us would admit to having if we were honest. The driven, watchful envy of a horizontal pleasure-oriented heart will make us crazy. It will not only rob us of our satisfaction and joy, but it will take our humanity from us and turn us into beastlike creatures. It will make us more like brutes than friends. It will eat our hearts and consume our souls.

Asaph's confession is insightful and indicting. It indicts us all, calling us to examine what separation from God and the resulting pleasure-oriented here-and-now envy does to each of us. If we fall into thinking that life is found in the pleasure and comforts of the people, things, and experiences of this here-and-now world, then that is what we will live for. We won't live for God. We won't first live for the good of others. We won't first be motivated by what is loving, good, true, and wise. No, we will live for ourselves, and whether we know it or not, every day we will be in hot pursuit of our private definition of pleasure. We will have ourselves at the center of our will. We will be our own kings and queens, seeking the control over people and circumstances that is necessary to ensure that we will, in fact, get the things we have set our hearts on. We become hyper-vigilant observers of our own lives and the lives of others. We become incessant pleasure/comfort accountants, measuring our experience of these things over against the experiences of those around us. We daily measure who has the biggest pile of pleasure, and we are unhappy if it is not us.

Like Asaph, we judge that we are more deserving than our comfortable friend, and we question the goodness of God and the moral good of obeying if at the end of the day we end up with the short end of the stick. The problem is not that we never do something loving, benevolent, or good. We do, but the core operating focus of our lives is us. What is the universal weakness of a human being? Selfishness. You see, we know that we are unhappy, but we tell ourselves that God has failed us and life has passed us by. We say that it is not fair that bad people get blessed while good people like us suffer through life with little. We struggle to hold on to our faith, wondering if what we have believed will be worth it all in the end.

The architecture of our lives is shaped by an infrastructure of personal expectations and self-focused demands. We know all too well what we want from people and situations, and we know what God needs to do in order for us to name him as good. What all this means is that at the deepest, profoundest, and most life-directing level of our hearts, we, like Asaph, have lost our senses. In the biblical sense of what the words mean, we have gone mad. The cancer of self-focused envy has simply made us crazy. Without realizing it, we have taken on a distorted view of reality. We have a distorted view of ourselves, others, life, and God.

You see, life will never operate the way we want it to. People will not submit to the laws of our kingdoms for long. God will not get up and give us his holy throne. Our reality is irrational and our hope is hopeless. Our dreams are gas (see Psalm 73:18–20). The more we work to fill our hearts, the emptier they become. The more we work to achieve our dreams, the more they vaporize in our hands. The more we live for ourselves, the more envious we become. It is socially acceptable madness. It cannot and will not ever work. This is not the way the world was created, and this is not who we were designed to be. We were designed to live with both King and kingdom consciousness, because we were designed to live for God. The architecture of our lives was to be shaped by all of the plans, purposes, words, and actions that would flow out of these words: "Your kingdom come, your will be done, on earth as it is in heaven" (Matthew 6:10). It is only inside of the boundaries of these words that true and lasting life and peace of heart will ever be found. Inside these boundaries, real wisdom and real love live. Inside of this moral structure, life lives in gorgeous beauty.

Outside are frustration, discouragement, anger, disappointment, and doubt. Sure, the temporary pleasures of here and now are enjoyable, but their shelf life is short. Creation has no capacity whatsoever to truly satisfy your heart. Your heart has been wired to find its hope, peace, and rest in God alone. What is spiritual death? It is living as if God doesn't exist. It is putting yourself where God is supposed to be.

Living for the pleasures of here and now as the principle quest of your life is a vain attempt to re-create the world and how it was designed to operate. No, it is not wrong to find pleasure pleasurable. It is not ungodly to desire comfort. It is not evil to desire good and loving relationships. It is not wrong to appreciate beauty. But here is what we need to understand: all of these things were beautifully designed by God to point and connect us to him. These created pleasures were not made to be an end in themselves, but a means to an end. All of creation is a finger pointing to the Lord of creation, in whom life can be found. Creation was made to introduce us to him over and over again.

The temporary pleasures of this present world are meant to point you to the lasting pleasure of knowing God. The rising of the sun each morning is meant to remind you of his faithfulness. The crushing power of a devastating storm is designed to make you reflect on his power. The sweetness of a human kiss is meant to remind you of his tender care. The dependency of the baby is there to remind you of your constant need of God. The fading beauty of the daffodil is meant to help you see his eternal beauty. The imperfect justice of the human community is designed to make you thankful that God is perfectly just. The tender moment of human mercy is there to cause you to rest in his mercy. That five-course meal is an opportunity to reflect on and be thankful for the spiritual food you need and that God graciously gives. The shifting stars in the night are created to remind you that Jesus is the Light that never shifts or fades. Every experience of love is meant to point you to his love. Every moment of grace is there to cause you to run to his grace. All of creation is a finger pointing to God. It was not meant to replace him.

Psalm 73 powerfully reminds us that this life is not all there is. The point of life is not personal, temporal pleasure. An end is coming. All that is now wrong will be made right. In pointing us to the final end of things, Psalm 73 tells us what the drama of life is all about. We were made to have God as the one life-shaping treasure of our hearts, but sin turns us in on ourselves. It causes us to forget who we are and that God exists. It turns us into little self-sovereigns, wanting to reign for our own glory.

SEEING DEATH AS PREPARATION

So the sad reality is that the ultimate interruption (physical death) and the ultimate separation (spiritual death) are all around us. No one has ever escaped, and no one ever will. We all come into this world dead (spiritually), and we will all die someday (physically). This really is the bad news you can't escape. Death is in the way of forever. It wasn't supposed to be this way, but it is the way it is now. How does the forever that was part of the original plan become your forever? How will forever be given back to people who were hardwired for forever? How will we be rescued from the insanity of trying to pack all our hopes and dreams into the here and now? How will we be protected from the drivenness, envy, and disappointment of living as if this is all there is? Where will we find peace of heart and life in this broken world that is now bracketed by death? Is there escape from the bad news of this double death?

The way for you to begin to experience real life is to face the inescapable reality of death. The death that is all around you is meant to get your attention. It is meant to force you to face the impermanence of the physical things around you. These things clearly have a limited and temporary ability to fulfill you. The wilting flowers, the rotting deck out back, and the food that quickly spoils are all meant to produce in you a deep hunger for life and for the forever that comes with it. Rather than depressing you, all of the death and impermanence around you is meant to open your eyes and inform your heart. It is meant to call you away from the delusion that this life is all there is and that you can find your identity, meaning, and purpose and your deepest inner sense of well-being from things that so quickly die.

Although it had taken awhile, Walter had begun to learn these lessons. He had spent much of his life disappointed, discouraged, and driven. Again and again, he had attached his identity, his inner sense of well-being, and his sense of the meaning of life to the situations, things, or people around him. Invariably, these things died. Friends moved away or failed to live up to Walter's expectations. His job turned out not to be his ticket to the good life. Fifteen years later, his new home was just another old home in need of repair. The dog, who probably was his best friend, died. When these things happened, Walter didn't get the message. He attached himself to some other impermanent part of the creation, only to be disappointed again. He didn't understand that the death around him was the ultimate clue that the way he was living would never work. Decaying creation would never be the messiah Walter hoped it would be.

The cancer and then death of a longtime friend were what finally opened Walter's eyes. His friend's death helped him see that the temporary things of this present world were not intended to be the place where he would find help, healing, and hope. It woke him up to the fact that since everything in creation is in the process of dying, he could not look there for life.

Facing the inescapable reality of death is what began to give Walter hope and peace. Does that sound strange to you? Here's how it works. When you work to deny the reality of death, you look for life in things that are dying—and that never works. Only when you face the bad news of death can you begin to find hope in the good news of life—life that begins in the here and now and lasts forever. This is what Jesus meant when he said, "Do not store up for yourselves treasures on earth, where moths and vermin destroy, and where thieves break in and steal" (Matthew 6:19).

Walter didn't just have death all around him; he had grace all around him as well. God, in grace, was using the disappointment of misplaced hope to lead Walter to where life could be found. When Walter began to look death in the face is when he began to be liberated from his bondage to the creation and began to find rest in the power, presence, and love of the Creator. Yes, Walter still felt the sting and pain of loss, but its power to paralyze him had been broken as he began to understand that he could not be robbed of life by something that was not designed to give him life.

Walter allowed the pain of death to be his teacher. Do we? We are being schooled. God wants us to learn from the inability of people, possessions, and experiences to satisfy our hearts. The message is clear and death is the giveaway: there has to be more than this life. God's plan is not for you to get as much as you can out of life and then die. Looking death in the face is meant to make you wise, and ultimately it is meant to give you peace. This is why God puts death in front of you so much. In grace God is working to rescue you from death and prepare you for forever.

Chapter Four

THE DARK SIDE OF FOREVER

Our son was just nine months old and from our vantage point, walking way too soon. Now that he was upright and mobile, a new world of danger awaited him. He seemed too young to be able to take in all the instructions and warnings we knew he needed, but we had to try. I walked him over to the electrical outlet and told him never to touch it or put anything in it. He wobbled back and forth and looked in every direction but the one toward which I was pointing. He gave me that "Are you done yet?" look. I warned him again, and then he toddled off to the next adventure in his tour of his newfound world.

The very next afternoon I was reading the paper in the living room, where we had had that cautionary conversation. As I read, I heard the pitter-patter of toddler feet coming down the hallway. My son peeked his head around the corner, not knowing that I could see him from behind the paper. Thinking I was otherwise distracted, he made a dash for the outlet, but before he reached for it, he turned back to see if I was watching. As he reached out his hand, I said a stern, "Justin!" and he began to cry.

The Dark Side of Forever

This was a sad but instructive moment for me. I couldn't believe the clarity with which I was seeing this living illustration. At only nine months old, my son had already bought into the deepest and darkest of all human delusions — one that grips every one of us, exposes the deepest desires of our hearts, leads us into danger, and causes much suffering in this world and in the one to come. What is this dark and dangerous dream? It is the belief, whether momentarily or lifelong, that what we choose to do or say doesn't really make any difference. It is the hope that there are no overarching moral laws, that every choice is not only possible, but reasonable. It is the hope that there is no such thing as cause and effect. It is the functional hope that life doesn't have any consequences. It is believing that I can do whatever I desire to do and things will be okay. It is the ultimate denial of reality, a rejection of the world as God made it. We may not self-consciously give in to this denial, but we all do it some way.

Denial of consequences is what leads the young student to think he can blow off his homework day after day and get away with no negative results. This delusion allows a person to think that she can eat whatever and whenever she wants and not face the physical consequences. It allows the adulterous husband to think he can manage his unfaithfulness and that his marriage will be okay. It allows the businessperson to cheat a little on her taxes and ignore the consequences. This delusion allows all of us to flirt with sin and not see danger coming. It enables many of us to spend more than we make and think things will be all right in the end. The reality is that all of us in some moment in our lives have thought that we could live outside of God's boundaries and that things would somehow work out. It is one of the ways we show how much we love to have our own way. In these times, we demonstrate that we think we are smarter than God, that our wisdom is greater than his, and that the boundaries we set for ourselves are better than the ones he has set for us.

Adam and Eve were the first to buy into this lie, and we have been doing the same ever since. In that fateful moment in the garden, they not only bought into the lie that disobeying God's clear command would be okay, but they also bought into the possibility that doing so would make their lives better. But it was not okay; the result was great harm to them and to the beautiful world God had made (see Genesis 3).

You won't understand this denial of the inescapable reality of consequences unless you acknowledge that it is rooted in something deeper—a rejection of the purpose for which each of us was created. We were not created for our own liberty, happiness, or fulfillment. We were not created to find our own way and to discover our own joy. We were not designed to define what our needs are and to give our lives to meet them. We were not made to treat the world like an endless buffet of delights for our consumption. We were made for God, made to live for his glory, and made to find the fullest expression of our humanity in loving, worshipful community with him. What Adam and Eve told themselves was more profound than "We can eat the fruit, and things will be okay." No, whether they were conscious of it or not, what they told themselves was, "We can choose to live for ourselves and not for God, and things will be okay."

Sin is much, much more than the breaking of a list of abstract laws. You'll see this if you examine the Ten Commandments (see Exodus 20). Sin is first the breaking of relationship with God. When we break relationship with God, we end up breaking his rules. Sin is essentially replacing God with other things as the center, the priority, and the primary motivation of our lives. This is why the first few commands on the list all have to do with loving and worshiping God. The rest of the list details all the areas in which we are tempted to replace God with something else or to do harm to someone who is in our selfish way. Every sin we commit is adulterous, because we are being unfaithful to the love relationship we were designed to have with God, and we are running into the arms of other lovers. The grand delusion of every act of sin is that we can be disloyal to God and everything will still work out in the end. (Read the graphic adultery imagery the Lord uses to describe the sin of Israel in Ezekiel 16.)

Every day billions of us get up and ignore the love relationship with God for which we were created. Because we do not love him as we should, we do not have the motivation to please him. Because we are not motivated to please him, we find it easy, in small moments and big, to replace him with something else. We replace love of God with a life-dominating love of self. We replace concern for the glory of God with self-glory. We replace a desire to serve the Creator in the way we steward his creation with the worship of the creation. Inserting ourselves in the center of our world is the ultimate delusion. Sin not only denies the structure of the world as God made it, but it also denies our very identity as human beings. We are God's image bearers. We were made for him. Living as if we are independent beings, free to live on our own and do our own thing will never work.

THE ULTIMATE CONSEQUENCE

The Bible has much to say about the consequences of our desires, thoughts, choices, words, and actions. Psalm 115 warns us against idolatry by telling us that we become like the idols we worship. "Those who make them will be like them, and so will all who trust in them" (v. 8). The person who worships material things becomes materialistic. The person who lives for control becomes controlling. One of the inescapable consequences of human life is that we all end up taking the shape of the things we serve.

The Bible also puts before us the word picture of planting and harvesting to remind us that our choices and decisions do make a difference. "Do not be deceived: God cannot be mocked. A man reaps what he sows" (Galatians 6:7). Every day each of us harvests what we previously planted, and we plant what we will someday harvest. We are all too skilled at denying our own harvest, but the

Bible is clear: God is not fooled; he knows that what we are now experiencing is directly connected to actions we have previously taken.

The Bible teaches two things that must be included in any book about forever. First, there will be a judgment of every human being who ever lived, and second, there is a place of eternal punishment for the wicked.

The Bible says that everyone will be judged. The writer to the Hebrews says that "people are destined to die once, and after that to face judgment" (Hebrews 9:27). Luke writes in Acts that "[God] has set a day when he will judge the world with justice by the man he has appointed" (17:31). And the apostle Paul says, "We must all appear before the judgment seat of Christ, so that each of us may receive what is due us for the things done while in the body, whether good or bad" (2 Corinthians 5:10). All who have ever lived will stand before the throne of God and give an account for the way they have lived and will hear God's final proclamation of the place of their eternal destiny.

The clear teaching of a final judgment is meant to be both a comfort and a warning to us. Perhaps you're thinking, *Paul, where in the world is the comfort here?* Hardwired into the heart of every human being is a desire for justice. Yes, sin has bent and twisted this desire, but it is there nonetheless. All of us have been or will be grieved by the lack of justice around us. Sometimes it seems like the bad guys are winning, like crime pays. In the here-and-now world we live in, right often doesn't get rewarded, and evil does seem to prosper. So we can take great comfort in knowing that God keeps accurate records and that ultimately the universe will be just because God is just. The final judgment assures us that all accounts will be settled, every wrong will be made right. The God who knows all and sees all will bring final justice to his world. To do anything less would be to deny himself.

But the Bible's frequent teaching of final judgment is also meant to be a constant moral alarm system for us. It is designed to screech louder than all the seductive voices that woo us into spiritual infidelity and rebellion. My brother Tedd, as the principal of a school, used to tell the teachers who were struggling with giving failing grades that if there were no such thing as failing, then passing wouldn't make any difference. If there is a final judgment, then what you do matters, forgiving grace is a necessity, and an eternal home with the Lord is a precious gift. The final judgment warns us against believing, even for a moment, that we live in an open universe where anything we desire is possible and potentially beneficial. Final judgment reminds us that we live in a moral world ruled by a holy God, who as Creator has the right to tell us how to live and to discipline us when we don't obey. Any other view of this world is a dangerous and destructive lie. So, like a loving father to his children, God points us to the future judgment again and again to protect us from buying into the lie. In love he says, "Please don't forget that someday you will stand before my throne and give an account."

The second thing the Bible teaches that must be included in any book about forever is the existence of a place of eternal punishment for the wicked called hell. The apostle Matthew pictures God saying to some, "Depart from me, you who are cursed, into the eternal fire prepared for the devil and his angels" (25:41). The apostle Mark recalls Jesus describing hell as a place "where the fire never goes out" (Mark 9:43). He adds that hell is a place "where the worms that eat them do not die" (v.48). Luke describes hell as a place of torment (16:23), and the apostle John adds that the smoke of this torment "will rise forever and ever" (Revelation 14:11).

Hell is the ultimate eternal consequence. If you live a life of unrepentant spiritual adultery, denying God's existence and glory and breaking his wise commands, you will spend eternity in hell. We cannot escape this teaching in the Word of God. We cannot do justice to the message of Scripture and ignore that there is a dark side of forever. The Bible clearly and repeatedly warns us so that each of us is without excuse. The warning itself is a demonstration of the love and grace of the one to whom we all are disloyal in some way.

What makes hell hell? Three things.

1. *Separation from God.* I don't know if I can provide the graphic description that everlasting separation from God requires, but I will try. Not enough has been written about this horror. It would be an existence far beyond any darkness that any human being has ever experienced. Every person, believer or unbeliever, benefits from the presence, power, and grace of God, for God's presence is what holds the world together and gives the world its order, beauty, and regularity. The sun that warms you and the breeze that cools you are signs of God's presence. The fact that you have water to drink and food to eat are the result of God's presence and control. God gives you breath and strength every day. He sustains your mental, emotional, spiritual, and physical capabilities. Even though we often are unaware of it, he guides and protects us every day. He sends the rain, he nurtures the flowers, and he is Lord over the storm. The regularity of all that makes up our existence as human beings and makes living possible is the result of his presence and his care. And he gifts us with all of these daily blessings that make life work even though we do not deserve them.

Imagine what would happen to the world if for just one moment God would withdraw his presence and his power. Everything around us would explode into utter chaos, and we would lose all ability to be the beings we were created to be. Now imagine the horror of the eternal chaos of living in a place completely separate from the presence, power, and grace of God. Imagine being in a place where nothing is what it was created to be; where there is no order, beauty, or rationality; where emotions have descended into unspeakable darkness; where there is nothing on which you can depend; where everything is completely broken and will never be restored; where every day is a horribly bad day and will never be followed by a better day; where beautiful things have become monstrous things; where everything and everyone is bent, twisted and distorted; where everything you lay your eyes on is a horror and there is no escape. Imagine the awfulness of God saying, "You have wanted to live separate from me your entire life, so you will now live in that state forever." Imagine the hell of separation from God.

2. *Inhumanity*. We were not created as independent, self-sufficient human beings. We were designed to live in a loving, worshipful, and dependent relationship with God. We are God's image bearers, designed to reflect his likeness. Our humanity reaches its fullest and most beautiful expression when we are living in close communion with the one who made us. Our humanity really is connected to his presence. The Bible describes the damage sin has wreaked on us in the present world this way: "They have become filled with every kind of wickedness, evil, greed and depravity. They are full of envy, murder, strife, deceit and malice. They are gossips, slanderers, God-haters, insolent, arrogant and boastful; they invent ways of doing evil, they disobey their parents; they have no understanding, no fidelity, no love, no mercy" (Romans 1:29–31).

Consider how far this description is from the beautiful humans beings God created in the garden of Eden. The King James Bible translates "no love" as "without natural affection." This is a description of the progressive loss of one's humanity. Those who persist in sin against God begin to lose the humanity of heart, the sensitivity of soul meant to protect and restrain every human being. They quit feeling things that human beings are meant to feel. Their hearts become hard and uncaring. What Paul is describing in this passage is prevalent in this present world. It is happening while God still exercises the restraint of his protective, providing, and order-producing grace. Imagine what human beings would become if every dark impulse was given free rein because the presence of God was totally withdrawn. Imagine living in a place where no good thing resides in anyone's heart. If nothing that makes human life human life can exist apart from the presence of God, what would happen if God was completely absent? Now imagine living in this state of dark inhumanity forever, and you are getting close to understanding one of the singular horrors of hell.

3. *Unending torment.* Because it is so easy for us to minimize our unfaithfulness to the relationship with God for which we were created, and because we daily step over God's boundaries, the torment of hell stands as a warning and protection for us. To come close to understanding the unending penalty for sin, we must stand at the intersection of the perfect holiness and justice of God and the enormity of the evil of sin. Our problem is that we have a perverse ability not to see sin for the huge evil that it is. In fact, we have the ability to look at sin and not see it as sinful at all. When we do this, we are in grave danger. The fact that we think eternal punishment is harsh and makes God less than fair demonstrates how far we have strayed from the biblical understanding of how evil evil is and how gloriously holy God is. Those who will experience eternal punishment will not do so because of an occasional breaking of God's law, but because of a lifelong, moment-by-moment rebellion against their Creator, a consistent desire to be in God's place, and an unyielding rejection of God's offer of rescuing and forgiving grace. Perhaps the biblical description of the torment of hell is one of the only accurate mechanisms we have been given to weigh the magnitude of the sinfulness of sin.

How should we respond to the Bible's message of the dark side of forever? The biblical teaching about hell should be hard for us. It should shake us. It should make us sad and uncomfortable. You should not be able to casually read what I have just described. The thought of suffering, let alone eternal suffering, should produce grief in your heart. If we still have tenderness in our hearts, we should wish that no one would ever experience eternal punishment. The thought that anyone would experience the unending, inhumane, God-separated torment of hell should produce agony in each one of us. It should also cause us to realize that what we do and say does make a difference. Hell is the ultimate reminder that we live in a moral universe under the care of a perfectly holy God. Any other view of the here and now is a delusion.

LIVING IN LIGHT OF THE DARK SIDE OF FOREVER

I will leave this look at the dark side of forever with practical directions on how to live in light of it in the here and now.

1. *Use every means available to fight the delusion that what you choose to do or say doesn't make any difference.* Every day you have to be willing to listen to the things you say to yourself as you interact with the temptation to step over God's boundaries. Are you one of sin's best salespersons, able to point yourself to sin's pleasure without ever mentioning its pain? Or are you one of sin's best watchpersons, always warning yourself that on the far side of God's boundaries is danger, destruction, and death? Fighting the battle of the denial of sin's consequences must become a lifelong commitment; you'll need to continue fighting until you're on the other side. A practical way to fight this delusion is to be in God's Word every day. The Bible is full of warnings and case studies that hold before the reader the bitter harvest of rebellion against God.

2. *Require yourself to see sin as sinful as it really is.* I will admit it, sin doesn't always appear sinful to me. Sometimes I am skilled at seeing beauty in what God says is ugly. Arguing my wife into a corner in order to get my own way sometimes looks more beautiful to me than living with her in the kind of self-sacrificing love to which God calls me. A brief moment of lust can look more attractive to me than the wholesome beauty of a pure heart. Being the center of attention can feel better to me than humbly pointing to God's glory in everything I do. I'm sure you have similar struggles.

If the dark side of forever reminds us of the evil of evil, then we must live with that same kind of seriousness in the here and now. We must prohibit ourselves from minimizing what God says is wrong, and we need to surround ourselves with people who encourage us to take God at his word. We need to look for those places where we think we are smarter than God and for the boundaries we set for ourselves that we think are better than the ones he has set for us. Since one of the principal tricks of the devil is to present sin as significantly more harmless than it is, the commitment to name sin as nothing less than evil must stay with us as long as sin is still inside us and outside temptations still call out to us.

3. *Be thankful for the final justice of God.* In our struggle with the unfairness and injustice of the broken world in which we live, it is important to remember that one day unrighteousness will end and all that is evil will be judged for what it is. Hell reminds us that there is a Judge of all things who keeps perfectly accurate records. No evil escapes his eye. He will never be tricked into seeing evil as good or injustice as just. The day will come when he will say, "Enough is enough," and will proclaim just judgment on all that is evil. Until then, we should be thankful that his justice waits and that each day he gives every human being one more opportunity to confess and repent.

4. *Celebrate forgiving grace every day.* Only when you acknowledge the sinfulness of sin and the coming doom of all who have been unfaithful to the service of the one who made them will you begin to celebrate the amazing grace offered to you through the life, death, and resurrection of Jesus. When you minimize sin, you will always devalue grace as well. All of us deserve the penalty of hell, but Jesus came to live the life we could not live and to die the death we deserved to die so that we might know God's forgiveness and eternal acceptance and escape the eternal doom of the dark side of forever. If you are God's child, you are still being rescued, forgiven, transformed, and delivered by that grace, and you will continue to be until forever with your Lord is your final home. Now that is reason to celebrate.

5. *Let the dark side of forever remind you of what is important.* What does hell tell us about what is important in the here and now? It tells us that nothing in life is more important than relationship with God. It tells us that pleasing God is more important than pleasing oneself. It tells us that all of God's commands, principles, instructions, directions, and comforts are more important than anything we could ever say to ourselves. Hell tells us that spiritual blessings are more important than physical pleasures. We can get so caught up in the world of physical locations, pleasures, and experiences that we lose sight of the fact that the most essential thing in life is living in daily communion with a God whom we cannot hear, see, or touch. The dark side of forever powerfully reminds us that there is nothing more important in all of life than to know, love, worship, and serve him.

Living in light of the dark of forever provides protection from temptation and leads us to celebrate the grace promised to all who have put their trust in Jesus, that they will never see the dark side of forever. The way we live really does make a difference.

Chapter Five

GRACE FREES US TO LIVE WITH ETERNITY IN VIEW

They were sad, distraught, and confused. They couldn't believe what they had just been through, and they didn't know what they would do now. They thought they had understood. They thought they had found what life was really all about. They just didn't expect it would end this way. They were going where they didn't want to go to see what they didn't want to see. Maybe grief drew them there. Maybe hope that what they knew was real wasn't real drew them. Perhaps they had a need to do the traditional things people did in a situation like this. Maybe they were drawn by deep love and respect, but whatever it was, nothing could prepare them for what they were about to experience.

When the disciples arrived at the tomb, they got the shock of their lives. Jesus was not there! For sure he was dead. The soldiers made certain of that, finishing him off with a sword. But the lifeless body wrapped in grave clothes that they expected to see was missing. What they saw made no sense, and as they stood there confused, two men in dazzling apparel appeared and told them something unthinkable, something that would change the world forever: Jesus was risen! *Risen?* What? When people die, that's it, isn't it? When the last breath rushes out of a person's body, life is over. We get up from a nap, we wake up after sleeping all night, we wiggle and awake when we've been dozing, but we don't get up from the grave and walk away. People who die stay dead!

But these two shiny men said something that didn't make sense: "Remember how he told you...," and immediately the disciples remembered. He had predicted that this amazing thing would happen, but it was so unimaginable that they hadn't taken it seriously. They ran to tell the others, but they didn't believe it either. It seemed that they were making it all up. Peter ran to check out this crazy tale, and to his amazement, he found the grave clothes there, but the body was gone. Maybe it was true! Could it actually be? Did he have that kind of power? Had death really been defeated? It was simply too much to take in (Luke 24:1–12).

Later that day, two of Jesus' followers were taking the seven-mile trek from Jerusalem to the distant suburb of Emmaus. Of course, with heads spinning and hearts hurting, they were trying to figure out all that had taken place in the last few days. As they were lost in conversation, a stranger joined them and asked what they were discussing so intently. They were surprised that this guy had no knowledge of the cataclysmic events of the last few days and concluded he must be a visitor. So they told him the story of Jesus' amazing ministry, his unjust sentence, and his cruel death. They shared that until all this had taken place, they had hoped that he was the one who would "redeem Israel." They went on to tell him of the mystery of the angels, empty tomb, and missing body.

What happened next was astonishing. The stranger said, "Don't you get it? This moment isn't the end; it's the beginning. God's plan was for the Messiah to suffer these things and then enter into his glory." Didn't they know that this was what all of the

Scriptures were about? And then at dinner the stranger revealed who he was: the resurrected Jesus (see Luke 24:13–35).

The God of forever, who created people to live with him forever, set in motion a plan to deal with death, the one thing smack-dab in the way of forever. To the one who is the Author of life, death is unacceptable. For death to be alive and well is not all right. For every human being to face and fear death is not okay. Nor is it acceptable for the spiritual death of separation from God and the physical death that ends every person's life to dominate the human story. This enemy of forever, this horrible intrusion, this painful interruption, must be defeated. Somehow death must be defeated. Death must die because it stands in the way of the forever we were created to enjoy. But there is nothing we can do about it. The story of the Bible is the story of God's doing the one thing we don't have the ability to do: kill death.

WHAT THE BIBLE IS ALL ABOUT

On that seven-mile walk, Jesus explained to his two confused followers what the Bible is all about: him. It is the story of his coming to earth to defeat sin and death and to restore forever to the creatures he made in his likeness. The Bible is not a book of moralistic insights to help us live our lives better, nor a compendium of sacred religious thought. The Bible is not a dictionary of human problems with the corollary divine solutions. It's not the history of how religion developed nor the rule book for being a good Christian. It is not about how to be good enough for God to like us enough to want to spend forever with us. The Bible is not a catalog of stories about noble people who made the right choices. The Bible is not an encyclopedia of theology for people who want to make sure they believe the right things.

Nor is the Bible a collection of religious short stories. It is one story from cover to cover with God's explanatory notes. It is the most amazing, radical, courage- and hope-giving story you could ever want to read. It is a story that is incredibly honest and tremendously hopeful at the same time. The plot will make you understand things you have never understood before and see things you would have been blind to. This story addresses your deepest questions and your fundamental fears. It has a shocking beginning, a horrible dilemma, an unexpected solution, and a glorious ending. It is the story of stories, the one story that every human being needs to hear and understand.

The story of the Bible is a death-and-life story. The stink of death and the fragrance of life are on every page. It can make you weep and celebrate. It can produce more sadness in you than you ever had and a deeper joy in you than you thought you could ever experience. In a real way, the Bible is all about the triumph of forever over the enemy of death. It is all about the reality that it would take the death of God's Son to get forever back again. A death would defeat death and give the one gift that had been lost but that no human being could get back again: life forever. Let me explain.

GETTING FOREVER BACK AGAIN

As we saw in chapter 3, Adam and Eve walked into what no human being was ever meant to experience: the double death of separation from God and physical demise.

The Bible has a name for what Adam and Eve did: sin. But it also tells us that sin is more than disobedient behavior. Sin is a condition of the heart that results in wrong behavior. This is why we can't defeat sin on our own. Sin is bigger than the things we do. Sin is about who we are, and because of who we are (sinners), we do the wrong things we do (sin). To defeat sin, we have to escape ourselves — something none of us is able to do. We step over God's behavioral boundaries because in our hearts we want our own way. We do what God calls us not to do because in our hearts we want freedom from any authority over us but our own.

69

We chafe against God's will because in our hearts we think freedom is found only in self-rule.

But Adam and Eve did not get the freedom and lasting pleasure buzz they thought self-rule would bring them. No, what they got was separation and death. The forever hardwired inside them now seemed unrealistic and unattainable, and death, which was once unthinkable, became a regular part of human existence. The world had been turned upside down. It seemed that forever had died forever, and no one on earth had the power to turn it all around again.

But what seemed to be the end of the story was not. God was not about to sit idly by as his world was turned upside down. The Creator of life was not about to be defeated by death. He would act. He would deal with death in the only way that would lead to its defeat. He had a plan. He would win. Forever would live again.

The world, invaded by death, was in a new state of chaos. Instead of people's lives being organized by love for God, they were driven by the constant pursuit of here-and-now pleasure. Death had invaded. The world had gone mad. But the story was not over, because God would not sit and watch the demise of his plan.

So God, in his grace, invaded our here-and-now madness in the person of his Son. Jesus did not transgress God's boundaries. He did not live for his own pleasure. He refused to ignore eternity. He lived a life that was perfect in his Father's eyes. But he did more; he willingly took the penalty of our selfishness on himself. On the cross he took our punishment and purchased our forgiveness. In Jesus, all who believe not only don't get what they deserve (condemnation), but they are also given what they have not earned (righteousness). Because of this forgiveness and righteousness, we are accepted into God's family forever. The crisis of the human existence is not that we are horizontally unfulfilled, but that we are vertically cut off. Grace connects us once again to God, and in so doing to the one place where our hearts can find rest and where we can be given back our senses. Grace not only connects us to God, but delivers us from ourselves and from the madness of our propensity to make life about little more than us in the here and now.

Grace gives forever back to us. We see that the promise of the cruel cross and the empty tomb is profoundly bigger than a happy life in the here and now. The promise of the empty tomb is that we will live with God forever. And in this way we are given back our humanity. Grace guarantees to all who place their faith in Jesus that forever is in their future. And what kind of forever? A forever that is not only free of punishment, but free of the madness of self-centered, pleasure-oriented here-and-now–ism, and the double death that goes with it.

One of the sweetest gifts of the cross of the Lord Jesus Christ is the gift of forever. It's something we can't earn but can graciously receive. When Jesus says that he came to give us life, he doesn't just mean meaningful life in the present. He also means *eternal* life. In purchasing for us life that goes on forever, Jesus not only gave us a future, but he also restored our ability to live as we were designed, with eternity in view. Most people think that living with eternity in view makes you a *spiritual* person, but living with forever in view is how God designed all human beings to live. Grace frees us from our bondage to the here and now and enables us to live in the freedom that only eternity can give.

The gift of eternal life is not just a gift for the future; it is a gift for the here and now. The forever life, which Jesus purchased by his life, death, and resurrection, begins now. Grace causes us to be alive to God and enables us to see spiritual realities to which we once were blind. So we don't load life on our shoulders as we once did, hoping we could exercise enough control over people and situations to make things work out okay. Instead, we live with the peace of knowing that a God of wisdom, power, and grace has already written the final chapter of our story. If he has already determined that we will live with him forever, will he not protect and provide for us along the way? The implications of this are life transforming. Let me explain.

When I think of living with forever in view, I think of how little we know about our own lives. None of us has fully understood our past, few of us really understand all that is happening in and around us in the present, and none of us has an accurate sense of what will happen tomorrow. No wonder so many of us are anxious and confused!

Do you remember the story of Joseph (see Genesis 37)? Joseph was the son of Jacob, and although he was the youngest in the family, he was going to get the principle inheritance (something normally reserved for the oldest son). His brothers hated him for being their father's favorite. They hated him even more when he told them he had a dream that seemed to say he would rule over them. In jealousy, they stripped him of the special robe his father had given him and sold him as a slave to merchants on their way to Egypt. The brothers then dipped Joseph's robe in goat blood and told their father that they had found Joseph's bloody robe but not him. And that's how Genesis 37 ends.

We tend to miss the drama of the moment because we know where the story goes next, but the characters in the story didn't. Jacob thought his son Joseph was dead (he wasn't). The brothers thought they had gotten rid of Joseph for good (they hadn't). Joseph thought he would die as a slave and never see his family again (he would not die as a slave, and he would see his family again). No one in this terrible family drama had a clue. The sense that all of them made of this dramatic moment was, in fact, nonsense.

We are just like Joseph and his family. We don't actually know as much as we think we know. The sense we make of our situation and relationships is often nonsense. The things we think are going to happen turn out to be very different from what happens. The moments we think are the end of the story turn out not to be the end, but a new beginning. That is why the gift of forever is such a precious gift for the here and now. We, who have been given eternal life, know where our story is going. Yes, we will be surprised by what is coming around the corner, but we know where our final destination is, and we know we will be cared for along the way. Peter describes all who have been given eternal life as those "who through faith are shielded by God's power until the coming of the salvation that is ready to be revealed in the last time" (1 Peter 1:5). We can live with mystery and we can live in the middle of things that we cannot control, because the gift of eternal life guarantees that we will be protected by God's power until forever is our final home.

Consider how this changes the way we think about and live our lives. If I am being protected by God's power, then I know that he will meet all of my needs. Freed from worrying about my needs, I am liberated from relationships that are shaped by demandingness and self-interest. This then frees me to give myself to love, to serve the people in my life. The grace of eternal life frees me from carrying the burden of having to convince myself and others that I am righteous. Eternal life means I have been forgiven, and since I have, God will never turn his back on me and walk away. I no longer have to live in guilt and shame. I no longer have to fear being known. I don't have to deny my weaknesses and failures. The gift of forever guarantees that I have been and will be forgiven and that everything that is broken inside of me will be completely repaired.

The grace of eternal life even changes the way I suffer. The belief that this present life is all I have makes suffering all the harder. You see, if present joy is all the joy I will ever have and someone takes it away from me, the impact is devastating. But if I know that this is not all there is, that God is moving me toward my final destination, then I know that this moment of pain is temporary. Living in light of eternity doesn't remove my pain, but it allows me to have hope in my moments of pain. This hope is rooted in the assurance that God has guaranteed me a future that will be completely devoid of the pain I am now enduring. On the other side, I will remember this time of suffering that I am now going through and that seems to be lasting forever as a flash of a moment. Paul says it is "light and momentary" (2 Corinthians 4:17) when compared to the eternal life of pain-free joy that I will experience forever.

But there is more. Living in light of forever means that I can wake up secure in the knowledge that it is impossible for me to ever be alone. The God of forever daily blesses me with his presence and his promises so that he will not lose me as I journey toward my final destination. This means it is also inaccurate for me to tell myself that no one cares for me or no one understands me. The gift of forever is not only about future hope, but also about God's presence and provision in the here and now.

Finally, the gift of forever means that I have been freed to approach life with joy. No, not joy because the people around me like me, or joy because my life is comfortable and predictable, or joy because my life has been free of suffering, but joy because I know that I have been given the best of gifts: the gift of eternal life. Grace has given me present provision and future hope, so I can live with joy even when the situations and relationships in my life are confusing and hard.

Marcus understood these things, and I felt privileged to be a witness to how it impacted the way he lived his life. Marcus was in the final stages of colon cancer. Only fifty-seven, he looked like he was ninety. His body had begun the process of shutting down. Marcus and his wife, Judy, knew that he didn't have much time. She held Marcus's hands and looked at him with the mature love of a woman married to her best friend. Marcus was quite alert for his condition, but he was neither angry nor afraid. Yes, he had moments of sorrow and pain. Yes, he hated the hospital and wanted to be home, but he complained little and he loved much. Marcus was more concerned with how his family was dealing with his suffering and impending death than he was about his own condition. He knew what was coming, and it gave him peace. Death at the cruel hands of cancer would not be the end of his life. Death would be the beginning of the life of his dreams. Finally free of his diseased and broken body, he would live forever as a whole and healthy man in a place free of the sorrow and suffering that was in that hospital room that day. I sat and witnessed the strength and hope forever can give to a suffering man.

That night I asked Judy how she was doing. She said, "Paul, years ago our marriage wasn't great, but by God's grace the last several years have been wonderful. I am going to miss Marcus more than I am able to express. I am sorry our daughters are going to lose their father so young. But I know this moment is not the end of Marcus's life. I know that in eternity this time will seem small. I don't want Marcus to have to suffer much longer. I am ready to say good-bye and send him to his final home." Forever kept Judy from the bitterness of feeling ripped off. Forever gave her joy when there seemed to be no place to look for joy. Forever gave Judy peace in the middle of life's hardest moment. Judy did not feel helpless and alone, because she looked at the hardest moment in her life through the lens of forever, and it changed everything.

Marcus's funeral is Saturday. There will be tears because he will be missed. But the sorrow will be harmonized by celebration. What will we celebrate? A promise made, a gift given, and a promise kept. Through tears of sorrow we will celebrate forever.

THE ADMISSION THAT LEADS TO SOLUTION

Many people are in desperate need of what they could never earn or deserve: the precious gift of life forever. They are walking around dead and don't even know it.

Perhaps I am describing you. In your heart you know something is wrong. All the busyness of your life hasn't resulted in the peace and rest you long for. You have lived a self-focused and shortsighted life. Maybe you're beginning to realize that forever teaches two life-shaping truths.

1. *Life is not all about you.* You are not in the center of your world now, and you won't be then. What makes eternity wonderful is that God is restored to his rightful place at the center of all things.

2. *Your heart will only be satisfied when it finds its satisfaction in God.* In eternity you will no longer search horizontally for what you will only find vertically. God is the pleasure in eternity that will make eternity pleasurable.

But there is hope. The God who lives at the center of everything is a God of glorious grace. And in grace he offers you freedom and a future. Perhaps this offer is best captured by the words a prophet wrote thousands of years ago. These words are alive with hope as much as they were the moment they were penned.

"Come, all you who are thirsty,
    come to the waters;
and you who have no money,
    come, buy and eat!
Come, buy wine and milk
    without money and without cost.
Why spend money on what is not bread,
    and your labor on what does not satisfy?
Listen, listen to me, and eat what is good,
    and you will delight in the richest of fare." (Isaiah 55:1–2)

This is a beautiful word picture. The picture of physical food is meant to point us to the reality of universal spiritual hunger. We all are born thirsty and hungry. So life is all about what we look to to fill us. In the middle of this invitation to eat and drink what is free is the ultimate question, "Why spend money on what is not bread, and your labor on what does not satisfy?" Sadly, many of us are doing this day after day after day.

Grace Frees Us to Live with Eternity in View

This invitation to "eat and drink" what you cannot earn is for you. But you have to admit your need and that there is nothing you can do to satisfy your need. Life forever is always a gift. It can't be earned. Perhaps you'd like to turn to the Giver and say something like this:

> *God, I've got it all wrong. I've put myself in the center of my world and written my own rules. I've acted as if this life is all there is and have been driven by the pleasures of the moment. So I need your help and forgiveness, but most of all I need you. I realize I need to be rescued from the death of separation from you in the here and now and from the death that separates me from the eternity for which I was created. I want to live for you, in you, and with you forever, and so in this moment I am seeking your grace. I gladly accept your offer of life now and life forever.*

Chapter Six

WHY IS FAITH SOMETIMES SO MISERABLE?

Scott got up to face another day. He liked much about his life, but one thing disappointed him. It nagged at him every day, capturing his thoughts in those quiet, private moments when he didn't want to think. His disappointment made him feel guilty because he was told he should be thankful, but he wasn't. Sundays were particularly hard. He dreaded them because he felt he had to put on his happy face and act as though things were okay with his heart when he knew they weren't. As he stood with his fellow Christians to sing familiar hymns and worship songs, his heart was more at war than at worship. The battle between faith and doubt raged every time. Scott wanted to believe the words he was singing, but they felt far from the realities of his life. The world of the hymns didn't look at all like the world Scott lived in, and that thought nagged at him.

As he listened to the preacher doing his thing, Scott would look around and wonder. Were other people where he was? Was he the only one with this struggle? Were others haunted by the questions that haunted him? Had he somehow missed the boat? Sunday after Sunday he got little from the sermon because he couldn't rein in his own mind. Scott knew something had to give, but he was afraid to admit how big his struggle was, let alone confess it to someone else. He was tempted to give up, to stop acting as if he believed something he doubted. Scott's faith was no longer a resting place. It was no longer joyful and motivating. Scott was a miserable Christian, but he had no idea how he had digressed from those early days of joy to where he now was. He wasn't about to sign up for functional atheism, but he knew his spiritual life wasn't working.

The thing that bugged Scott was the contrast between the promises of the gospel and the reality of his life. Yes, he had a good job; yes, he was thankful for his wife and children; and, yes, he hadn't faced the kind of suffering he knew others had, but his life was full of prayers of hope followed by moments of disappointment. Scott loved Cassie, but marriage was hard. Rare was the day when they did not have some kind of disagreement or misunderstanding. His job was well paying and secure, but he had days when he dreaded going to work. He hated the competitive environment, and he was tired of being passed over for the next promotion just because he was unwilling to "kiss his boss's behind" like some of his coworkers did. Scott was constantly overwhelmed with parenting. Just when he began to feel that he had caught up with and understood his children, they would be off to the next stage of their development. He was weary with the constant squabbles and endless demands. On his drive home at the end of the day, Scott wasn't always excited to see his family.

No, his life wasn't marked by pain and suffering; it was simply harder day by day than he ever thought it would be. He would say again and again, "This isn't the 'abundant life' I thought I signed on for." Or, in a moment of difficulty, he would think to himself, *Where are all those promises now?* Scott was miserable, and he didn't know how not to be.

Scott is not alone. I am convinced that there are thousands of sad, defeated, disappointed, doubting, and soon to be cynical, Christians out there. Most are still going to church. Most are still participating in the externals of Christianity, but their faith no longer brings inward peace and outward motivation to the interior of their lives. They are going through the motions, but the life is gone. Their faith doesn't make sense to them anymore, but they simply lack the courage to admit it.

THE SIGNS OF A MISERABLE FAITH

Do you have a miserable faith? Sadly, many people do, and they don't even know it. Here are the signs:

1. *Disappointment with God.* There are more professing believers that are disappointed with God than we think. Because we don't look at life from the perspective of eternity, we misunderstand what God is doing in the here and now. The result is that we think he has not given us the life that he has promised.

2. *Lack of motivation for ministry.* If you are not excited about and thankful for the life that God has given you through the resurrection of his Son, you certainly won't be excited about sharing that life with others. A life of vibrant ministry is not the result of ministry training, but the result of a deep conviction that God is who he has said he is and is doing all that he promised to do. Ministry always flows from a thankful heart.

3. *Numbing.* When you're disappointed with your life, you will find ways to escape it. That may come in the form of busyness. You fill your schedule to the brim to keep yourself from having a moment to think. Or you may try to escape by watching way too much television. You're watching not because you're addicted to the content before you, but because you're addicted to the escape

that content provides for you. Or you may try to flee life by spending endless hours on the Internet, in the dark escape of the buzz of pornography, or in the temporary pleasure of too much food or alcohol. Maybe your escape is a hobby, sport, or outdoor activity. The point is that you are either facing life with hope and courage or you are finding a way to escape it.

4. *Envy of others' lives.* When you're disappointed with your life, it is tempting to scan the lives of others and see how they're doing. Invariably you will find someone near you who is enjoying the things that seemed to pass you by. It's hard in these moments not to wish you could exchange addresses with them. It's also hard to accuse God of getting the wrong address. Envy always doubts God, and envy always assumes someone else is getting what you deserve. But most of all, envy forgets eternity and only measures life by what is happening right here, right now.

5. *Letting go of the habits of faith.* When you're disappointed with something, you don't want to invest in or participate in it. Why read God's Word, why pray, why hang around with other believers, why read good Christian books, and why encourage others to believe when none of those things seem to make a difference? You're convinced your faith isn't working, and that makes pursuing it further very difficult.

6. *Greater susceptibility to temptation.* When my faith is exciting and precious to me, the things that would woo me away are not as attractive as they are when my faith doesn't seem to be working. When I am disappointed with God, it is much easier to step outside of his boundaries.

The promise of forever is that you don't have to live this way. Surety is rooted in the knowledge that everything that is broken will be restored and renewed, and that you will live forever with God in that renewed world.

THE DIFFERENCE THE HOPE OF FOREVER MAKES

First Corinthians 15 is perhaps one of the most foundational chapters in all of the New Testament. It is Christianity 101. The apostle Paul speaks to the Scotts of the world and their miserable faith. Read the following words carefully:

> But if it is preached that Christ has been raised from the dead, how can some of you say that there is no resurrection of the dead? If there is no resurrection of the dead, then not even Christ has been raised. And if Christ has not been raised, our preaching is useless and so is your faith. More than that, we are then found to be false witnesses about God, for we have testified about God that he raised Christ from the dead. But he did not raise him if in fact the dead are not raised. For if the dead are not raised, then Christ has not been raised either. And if Christ has not been raised, your faith is futile; you are still in your sins. Then those also who have fallen asleep in Christ are lost. If only for this life we have hope in Christ, we are of all people most to be pitied. (vv. 12–19)

Paul's argument is simple and clear: without eternity Christianity makes no sense. If all that sin has broken won't be forever fixed someday, then there is no hope now and no hope in the hereafter. What Paul says here is radical: without a guaranteed forever, faith in Christ is robbed of its meaning, power, and hope. I don't think I could say it more forcefully than he does: "If only for this life we have hope in Christ, we are of all people most to be pitied." Why? Because we have placed our hope in something that doesn't offer us any hope, because it doesn't guarantee the one thing that the world and every person who has ever lived in it needs: radical and complete renewal.

Let's work through Paul's logic. Our hope for the future depends on the actual point-in-time historicity of a past event, on the actuality of the resurrection of Jesus. If there was no empty tomb, then there is no hope of life after death. In order to offer us life after death, Jesus had to defeat death. Life with God forever guarantees our final deliverance from all that sin has broken and life forever with the Lord. If Jesus did not rise from the dead, then we are stuck in our sins and the hope of forever melts away.

Paul goes on to give this beautiful word picture: "But Christ has indeed been raised from the dead, the firstfruits of those who have fallen asleep." I remember planting our first vegetable garden with our kids. We dug long and straight furrows to put in seeds that would result in beautiful, crisp green beans at harvesttime. We carefully covered over the furrow with rich, dark soil and watered all the way down the line. The next day our children ran out to see the beans, but there were none. They had to learn the patience of a gardener. I will never forget the first sight of an actual baby green bean. We celebrated together although we had not yet eaten one green bean. Why? Because we knew what this firstfruit meant. That baby green bean was a promise of more to come.

Similarly, Jesus' earthly resurrection was not intended to be just the first resurrection, but the first in a line of future resurrections. His resurrection guarantees the final resurrection of all who believe. It says that the one thing between you and me and forever—death—has been defeated, giving back the hope of forever to all who have placed their trust in Jesus. Jesus defeated death, and so will you if you are his child.

Here are some specific ways the resurrection makes a difference in the here and now:

1. *The resurrection of Jesus and the hope of forever tell us what is really important in life.* Many of us have lost sight of what is truly important. Consider these examples:

- Sarah lost it yesterday morning when her son spilled his cereal for the third day in a row.
- Sam silently cursed the weather that had created the traffic jam that he didn't want to be in.

- Mary didn't seem to be able to quit obsessing over the fact that Susan hadn't asked her to be in her wedding.
- Frank struggled with being bitter that as a father of four he had little time for himself anymore.
- Jeanna was tired of having to pick up after her roommate.

When circumstances rise to levels of importance way beyond their actual importance, they exercise more control over us than they should. Success is not the most important thing in life. Pleasure is not the most important thing in life. The degree to which others appreciate us and accept us is not the most important thing in life either, nor is the degree of our control over people and circumstances or the size of our pile of possessions. The resurrection of Jesus and the hope of forever give us a sense of priority and proportion.

The most important thing in life is that we have help with and victory over our biggest and most abiding problem. What is that problem? Well, it's not your neighbor who is so hard to get along with, or your boss, who never seems to give you credit. It's not your finances, which always seem to get the best of you, or your children, who seem so hard to parent. It's not your spouse, who seems to be in the way of what you dream your marriage could be. It's not the fact that your house seems to be in constant need of maintenance or your car in regular need of repair.

As I have written and will continue to write, your biggest difficulty is not outside of you, *it is inside of you*. The Bible names it: sin. The resurrection of Jesus and the hope of eternity are a necessity because the sin inside you is an inescapable reality. You take it wherever you go. It separates you from relationship with God and puts you in dysfunctional relationships with others. Sin distorts your thoughts and kidnaps your motives. It makes it impossible for you to be what you were created to be and to do what you were created to do. Sin leaves you guilty before God and facing death. It is the universal and unavoidable disease. It is the one thing we cannot rescue ourselves from. It is the one place in life where we are completely powerless and utterly hopeless. It destroys our spirituality as it robs us of our humanity. If you are living for all those other things and are ignoring your sin, you are ignoring the single most significant problem of your existence. The resurrection of Jesus and the hope of eternity point to what is really important, to what you really need.

Sure, all those relational, situational, and physical things you worry about are important in some way, but they must not be viewed as the essence of what life is about. Paul is saying that without the resurrection, Christianity is a sham, because it offers us no help with the central, most important issue of life: sin. The resurrection guarantees the progressive defeat of sin in the here and now and the final deliverance from it in eternity. No human need is more profoundly significant in every way than the defeat of and deliverance from sin.

Many of the things we fret and obsess about just aren't as important as we make them to be. It really isn't that important that your neighbor has stolen six inches of your property for his rosebushes. It isn't that important that your teenage son has what appears to be a rather ridiculous looking haircut. It isn't such a big deal that your spouse is sloppier than you wish he would be. It isn't that important that you didn't get the office you thought you deserved more than your coworker did. In the scheme of things, that daily traffic isn't worth the emotional toll that you let it take on you. And the list could go on.

Let's return to Scott. He was confused about what God was doing, and because he was, he lived with unrealistic expectations, which resulted in disenchantment with his faith. What Scott failed to understand was that the life that God promised him and was delivering to him was not the good life of an easy, predictable marriage, compliant children, and a satisfying job. God promised to work on Scott. Every day Scott was the recipient of patient, forgiving grace. Every day he was given the power to defeat temptations that he could not defeat on his own. In situation after situation, God was using the difficulties of life to grow, change, and mature Scott. On all of those days when Scott felt abandoned and alone, he was being loved by God. All of those promises that Scott doubted were being fulfilled daily, but not in the way he expected or in the places he looked.

God was with Scott, in Scott, and for Scott, but Scott didn't see it because he didn't view his life from the vantage point of the resurrection of Jesus. The resurrection assures us that God will ultimately defeat our biggest enemy: sin. What Scott didn't understand is that this defeat is a process that begins in the here and now and stretches to forever. Scott didn't need to look for life in a good marriage, compliant children, and a fulfilling job, because he had already been given life. Yes, his life was rocky at times; however, those moments weren't a failure of God's plan, but a tool in his hands. The most important gift of all, the defeat of sin, was being delivered to Scott, but he didn't see it. Scott was being given the good life, yet day after day he awoke to the disappointment of believing that the good life had passed him by.

By grace, Scott began to see and understand. He began to realize that he had looked for life where it would never be found. And because he had done this, things became more important to him than they really were. But Scott began to understand what God was doing. I remember Scott saying, "I know my marriage isn't all that it could be, my children are difficult at times, and my job isn't always fulfilling, but I have reason to be thankful and encouraged. I am so thankful for the hope that the resurrection gives me today and will give me forever. Today, because of the resurrection, I am given forgiveness for my wrongs, power to face temptation, and the hope that one day my battle will be over. And I also know that when things are tough, God is not absent, but using hardship to make me a man who quits looking for life where it can't be found and who starts celebrating the life he has already been given and the life that is to come." Because Scott now gets what God is doing, he approaches his marriage, parenting, and job with peace of heart and confidence in the presence and help of the resurrected Jesus.

2. *The resurrection of Jesus and the hope of eternity have the power to radically change the way you approach the responsibilities, difficulties, and opportunities of your daily life.* Notice how Paul ends his discussion of the first and the final resurrection. "Therefore, my dear brothers and sisters, stand firm. Let nothing move you. Always give yourselves fully to the work of the Lord, because you know that your labor in the Lord is not in vain" (1 Corinthians 15:58). These are exciting words. What Paul is essentially saying is that eternity takes the vanity out of your living in the here and now.

So how can that knowledge change our approach to life? It means we have reason to continue. That's what it means to be steadfast. We don't continue because we can see that our efforts are bringing us success or because we are being affirmed by others. We don't continue because we can see how our problems will be solved. We don't continue because continuing is pleasurable. We continue because we get the plan. We continue because we know that grace has given us a life beyond this life, and the forever that is before us makes the things we do in the here and now meaningful and consequential.

Moreover, we become a person who isn't easily moved or sidetracked. Many people give themselves to something that they are convinced is right, but they quickly give up in the face of difficulties or obstacles. Sometimes it's not even big things that make people wonder if it's worth it. No, often it's the little nagging difficulties that get them down and move them off track. The reality is that between here and forever there will always be little and big things in the way. The world we live in is a broken place not operating as it was designed to operate. In case you hadn't noticed, people are less than perfect. Add to this the fact that God has planned for us to live right where we are living so that we would be made ready for what comes next. For these reasons, we will not live lives where we are able to get from point A to point B unobstructed.

87

This means that, in the here and now, we had better have a grander motivation when we get up in the morning than the hope that our day will be predictable, easy, and relatively free of hassle. Eternity gives us just that kind of big-picture motivation. We stay focused on doing what is good, right, and true, not because in the short term it appears to be working, but because our living in the here and now fits with the big plan of what God is doing and where he is taking us. In the face of hassles, we tell ourselves that this is not our final destination. We constantly reassure ourselves with the reality that we are on our way to a place where there will be no more sin, suffering, chaos, confusion, hurt, brokenness, or disappointment. But if this life is all there is, and this isn't working, then what motivation do I have to continue? I have to have something bigger than me against the world. That's why Paul ends his discussion of the resurrection of Jesus and the promise of life after death the way he does. Paul knows that in conquering death, Jesus has not only purchased for us the guarantee of life *after* death, but also the reality of life *before* death, a quality of life that wouldn't be possible apart from the new life the resurrection of Jesus delivered.

Now, all the things you do that are shaped by your belief in forgiveness now and for eternity are infused with new purpose, new meaning, and new hope. You are freed from wondering what in the world is going to happen to you and where in the world your life is going. You have been rescued from trying to control what you cannot control. You are delivered from tying all of your deepest hopes and dreams to temporary and dysfunctional situations and relationships. You no longer have to search for identity in things that were never designed to give you identity. The resurrection of Jesus, its guarantee of a final resurrection to come and the forever that will follow, defines who you are, what you need, what your life is about, and where you are going. Now everything you do is connected to a radically different present and a guaranteed future. All the things that are unsure in your life are now connected to things that are sure. All the things that you would wonder about are connected to things that you know for sure and can bank on. Eternity changes the whole game.

3. *The resurrection of Jesus and the hope of eternity teach you delayed gratification.* Western culture is not a waiting culture. We sigh when we get to Starbucks in the morning and there's a bit of a line. We drum our fingers on the desk as we impatiently wait the seven seconds it takes for the webpage to load. We hate even the thought of being stuck in traffic. We are an instant culture. But the hope of forever calls us to a different worldview.

In God's plan, waiting is not an interruption or obstruction of the plan; waiting is part of the plan. As we are waiting for the forever that is the promise of God's grace, we are not just marking time. From an eternal perspective, waiting is about becoming. When Adam and Eve disobeyed, God immediately put in place a process that would result in redemption and restoration. God is progressively transforming us into what he created us to be, and he is preparing us for the eternity that is to follow. By his grace, every moment of waiting is, in his hands, an efficient tool for personal restoration and preparation.

Isaiah 61:3 beautifully captures this process: "They will be called oaks of righteousness, a planting of the LORD, for the display of his splendor." These words capture God's plan for each of his children and what he is working on in the time between the fall in the garden and the forever he has promised. And what is that plan? That you and I would be as strong and as durable through the seasons and storms of life as the mighty oak tree is. The things that the oak endures season after season are the things that contribute to its grandeur and strength. Oak trees don't sprout up and mature overnight. It takes scores of years to bring a mighty oak to maturity, but when it is mature, it lives with a strength and splendor that few plants in God's creation have.

Notice that the prophet Isaiah didn't write that God was working to make us toadstools of righteousness. A toadstool sprouts up overnight, but you can uproot it with a flick of your finger. God is calling us to live through seasons of redemptive process so that we will be people of enduring strength and character whose lives point to God's glory and who are ready for the forever that he has promised to his children.

DEEPENING YOUR GRASP ON THIS UNSHAKABLE REALITY

Pay attention to what I am about to say. Ask yourself how your faith is doing. If you name yourself to be a Christian and you say that you have placed your trust in Jesus but are living in the here and now as if nothing in your life is sure, you have a miserable faith. You have put your faith in Jesus only to have your life end up being harder than it ever was. Surety, which will not be weakened or victimized by the trials of life, comes only as the result of a deep grasp of the unshakable reality that there will be a final restoration of all that sin has broken.

Maybe as you're reading this you're thinking, "Paul, I don't think I have this conviction in the way you describe it, and I don't know how to get it." I want to suggest some things. First, admit your need to God. He will always respond in grace to those who come to him with their struggle to live in light of what he says is true. Next, I would suggest that you get a good Bible commentary and spend some time studying 1 Corinthians 15. God's Word has the power to alter the way you think, and in altering the way you think, change the way you view life, and in changing the way you view life, begin to change the way you live it. Third, become more aware of the things you say to yourself. You are in a constant conversation with yourself, so the things you tell yourself are important and formative. If you tell yourself often that you are alone, that life has passed you by, and that God's promises are not true, soon you will believe these things. Fourth, seek the company of people who have the very certainty you lack. This kind of fellowship is an important instrument of change in God's hands. Finally, look for reasons to be thankful and encouraged. Instead of assuming you have missed life, look for signs of life. Instead of assuming that God is absent, look for his presence. Instead of assuming that God's promises have failed, look for signs of the good things he has promised. Celebrate life even when you don't see it, knowing that your problem isn't that God is absent or unfaithful, but that there are times when all of us simply don't see him very well.

If you're struggling with a miserable faith, don't run from God; run to him. He understands your struggle, and he alone can offer you the life that holds the promise of the resurrection and the hope of forever.

Chapter Seven

HOPE CAN'T LIVE WITHOUT FOREVER

You do it in grand moments of choice that are more deeply theological than you know, and you do it almost unconsciously every day in a myriad of seemingly spontaneous decisions. As you do it, you are setting the direction of your life, committing to a basic system of values and determining the shape of your principal relationships. You can't live without it, and when you have it, you want it to be real and reliable. You look up to people who are full of it, and you pity people who have none. No one wants to be without it. What am I talking about? *Hope.*

Think of all the things you hope for in a given day. You hope the traffic won't make you late. You hope your report at work will be well received. You hope your friend will understand why you didn't go to her party. You hope the weather won't cancel your flight. You hope you'll have enough money to cover all your bills. You hope your children will grow up to be what they were meant to be. You hope you'll find a good church in the city to which you just moved. You hope that cyst the doctor discovered isn't cancerous. You hope you can solve the problems in your marriage. You hope your insurance will cover the damage on your car. You hope you can defeat the fear that seems to hold you back. You hope you can become more of a person of faith. You hope you will hear something on Sunday that will leave you encouraged. You hope your son will be safe and make good choices at his new university. You hope your daughter will realize that her new man is not the man for her. You hope that what you believe will be proven to be really and finally true. You hope that God is all he has said he is, and that all his promises will prove to be true.

Hope is one of the most formative quests of the human existence. It is an inescapable quest, a daily preoccupation, and a lifelong journey. We all search for, long for, and attach ourselves to some kind of hope. We hook our hope to something, get disappointed, and shop for hope again. The thing we place our hope in will influence the way we interpret and respond to life. Hope is one of the most important lifelong journeys for every human being. For most of us, although we may not be conscious of it, hope isn't a settled thing, but a search. In this way hope is both a verb and a noun. It is the thing I am doing as I journey through life—I am hoping to find something to hope in, and it is the object of my journey.

Like everyone you know, you want something to hook your hope to. In fact, you are always hooking your hope to something or someone. Hope gets us up in the morning and puts us to sleep at night. It's what gives us courage to continue and reason to let something go. It enables us to stare difficulty in the face and not give up. Our biggest celebrations and our deepest sadnesses are connected to hope. Here is the problem: most of the things we hope in and hope for will disappoint us. The reason is simple and clear: *if your hope is not connected to forever, your hope will somehow die.*

Living with forever in view gives you an unshakable reason for hope. No matter how confusing life is, no matter how difficult the moment you're in is, no matter how forsaken you feel, no matter how much you may be overwhelmed by what is on your plate, and no matter what is down the road for you, you have reason for hope. Grace has purchased a forever for you that is beyond your wildest dreams. If you are God's child, you really do have reason for hope!

LIVING IN A DISAPPOINTING WORLD

We live in a disappointing world. Admit it. It will do you good. Many of your hopes for this life have been disappointed. Perhaps your job hasn't turned out to be all that you had dreamed it could be. Maybe the expected raise never happened, the promotion evaporated with the melting economy, your boss didn't turn out to be such a nice guy after all. Your house hasn't turned out to be the "perfect home for us" that you anticipated. It was tough for you to deal with the reality that you had major plumbing problems or that your commute turned out to eat up more of your day than you calculated it would. You have had days when you have felt distant from your spouse, when you were hurt by what the other person said or did, or when your marriage took more work than you ever thought it would.

Your church has disappointed you too. Sometimes you're not too excited about another Sunday morning. You're tired of the same old religious routine and wonder if you're alone in your middle-of-the-service boredom. You've thought of searching for another church, but the prospect of that seems overwhelming.

Your possessions have disappointed you as well. That living room set that seemed so comfortable and cool now looks tired and outdated. Those cutting-edge appliances now seem like antiques. Your new car has become the used car that you wish you had dumped before it entered its present stage of unpredictability.

Maybe you're even disappointed with you. In your honest moments, you look back on your life with loads of regret. You never did become the attentive dad you planned to be. You became a much more legalistic and demanding mother than you ever intended to be. You never did institute those yearly family traditions you thought would create great memories for your children. Perhaps you're only thirty-five, but you are already disappointed at the way you've let yourself go physically. You keep saying you'll eat better and exercise more, but your moments of health reformation are more moments of guilt than habits of change.

Your government has disappointed you. That mayor who you thought would bring in a new day has proven to be another unqualified political hack. Your government seems to be intent on taxing you into oblivion, and the schools you send your kids to don't seem equipped to give them the education they need to prepare them for life. You're tired of driving on overcrowded roads that seem to be in a terminal state of disrepair. Your national leaders seem more intent on building and protecting personal political power than serving the needs and concerns of their constituents. The cost of medical care increases your fear of getting sick, and your doctor seems so driven by the size of her caseload that she seldom spends more than a few minutes per visit with you.

Most of the things we hope in and for don't have much of a shelf life. Most of us are just around the corner from having our hope shattered. We are more hopeless than we think we are, and we are hopeless because we have detached our hopes from eternity. We load all our hopes and dreams onto the temporary shoulders of the situations, locations, and relationships of the here and now. We bounce from hope to hope, hoping that the things we are now placing our hope in won't fail us like the things we last hoped in did. So we go into a new marriage holding on tightly to the hope that it will deliver in ways that the last one didn't. We're excited about the new job because it looks as though it will surely be what the last job wasn't. The new diet has us excited because it is more balanced than the previous one that failed us. We're pumped about the new house, which we are sure was constructed better than the previous house, which seemed as if it was going to fall down around our feet. We're enthusiastic about the new church.

We've heard so much about the pastor and the amazing Sunday worship services. We're even excited about the new mall with the kind of flagship stores that have a wider range of products.

We careen from dashed hopes to hopeful hopes over and over again in an endless quest to have a reason to get up in the morning and continue. We are hope junkies. We want hope, and we refuse to live without it. But at the same time, we put our hope in places that can't give us lasting hope, and this only leads to one place: disappointment and ultimately hopelessness.

SO WHAT IN THE WORLD IS HOPE?

I don't want to take for granted that we are on the same page and have the same definition of hope. The following story illustrates how hope functions in most people's lives.

John was dissatisfied. He didn't always think about it, but when he did, he felt as if something was missing. Sure there were many good things in John's life, but it still felt a bit empty. He had a good job and a comfortable life. He had some good guys to hang out with and had explored a lot of places with his mountain bike. He was fit and healthy. But nights were hard for John. He felt lonely after his day of work and at times wondered if it was all worth it. He often stayed out later than he needed to just to avoid the quietness of his condo.

Things changed when John met Melinda. She was active, energetic, and fun. She was also intelligent and spiritual. The bonus was that she loved to go mountain biking. John and Melinda connected through their interests and spirituality. In ways John hadn't experienced in a while, Melinda made him feel alive. She became the reason John woke up excited about the day and the reason he wanted to be successful at work. She became the reason he wanted to go to church, stay healthy, and be financially solvent. She became the reason John laughed and the occasion for him to think more seriously than he had ever thought before. Melinda became John's primary activity and his constant preoccupation. She supplanted most of his friendships and was the reason he spent most of his money. Nothing in John's life loomed larger than Melinda, and that is just the way John wanted it. The day after their wedding, John couldn't believe that he would get to spend the rest of his life with her.

John didn't know what had happened inside him, but he was living with more hope than he ever had before. All he knew was that he loved where his life was going—until Melinda got sick. It didn't seem much to be worried about at first. She began to have trouble keeping up with him on their mountain-biking trips and seemed tired most of the time. But she had been working hard and carried the stress of lots of responsibility at work. When her exhaustion didn't pass, John suggested that she get a thorough physical. The doctor discovered that Melinda had an auto-immune disease that would be long-term and progressive. That's when John's world of hope began to crumble. Melinda was not going to die anytime soon, but it was clear that the life John had expected to have with her would never happen. Not only would she be unable to participate in the activities they both loved, but he too would have to give them up because he would spend much of his time caring for Melinda's needs.

For the next few weeks after the diagnosis, the alarm in the morning seemed like John's mortal enemy. He would hear it and be filled with a toxic cocktail of dread, fear, and anger. Work and church seemed meaningless, and he was tired of answering questions about Melinda's condition and prognosis. It all seemed a cruel joke. He wanted to believe it was a bad dream and he would wake up at some point. But it was not a dream. John was being confronted with the temporary nature of horizontal, here-and-now hope, and he was crushed.

Embedded in John's story is a street-level, functional definition of hope. *Hope happens at the intersection of desire and expectation.* Hope is a wish for something that is attached to a confident expectation that the wish will be fulfilled. Hope always has a *desire* and an *object* of that desire. You dream for something, and you place the fulfillment of that dream in the hands of something. Isn't this exactly what John did? He had a dream of a better, more pleasurable, and more satisfying life (*desire*), and he put that dream in the hands of Melinda (*object*). The problem was, both sides of John's hope were doomed to fail him. Let me explain.

John's hope disappointed because it was placed in temporal things. His hope was devoid of forever. It was completely a "got to have it here and now" hope. There was no sense of delayed gratification in John's dream. He loaded all his personal motivation and meaning and purpose into the experiences and relationships of this present world. When his dream didn't materialize in the here and now, his life lost its meaning. He had no sense that what he was facing was a preparation for a destination to come. He failed to recognize that God was using this hardship to teach him the temporary nature of all the things people placed their hope in in this present world and was calling him to look for a deeper, more reliable hope. God was calling him to put his hope in him: just what he would do when forever became his final home. But John treated now as a destination, and he knew exactly what he wanted it to look like. His was a dangerous and an almost always disappointing way of looking at the world.

John's problem was not just the desire that fueled his hope, but the object of his hope as well. Think about it: John placed his life in the hands of Melinda. Let that sink in. She became the carrier of John's dream, and in being the carrier of John's dream, she became the central object of his hope. There was no way she could pull this off. If sickness hadn't robbed her of her ability to carry John's dream, some other form of human frailty would. John asked Melinda to be his own personal messiah, to give him peace, meaning, and hope. And in a terrible encounter with the brokenness of the world, John was confronted with Melinda's fundamental inability to deliver.

Now, I don't want to give the impression that it is wrong to dream, wrong to hope, or wrong to wish that things were better. If you are alive and well, you are putting your hope in something. You don't live by animal instinct, because you have a heart. Your heart, the seat of your thoughts, desires, emotions, values, and choices, is your directional system. Everything you do is the expression of certain thoughts and certain desires. All of your little choices and major decisions in life are rooted in desire and are also an expression of some kind of hope. God hardwired you to operate this way. So you make daily hope investments, most of them of little notice and some of major consequence.

Something else is going on in your world of hope: longing. Hope is rooted in longing. I'll say it again: deep inside you is a longing for the return of the paradise for which you were created, a paradise that was to last forever. So, wherever you are, you are able to envision something better. Now maybe your better wouldn't really be better, or maybe your better is a self-focused version of better, but in some way we human beings are just a bunch of dreamers longing for a better world. So it's not wrong to hope; it's just that hope will always disappoint unless it is attached to forever.

WHERE HOPE CAN BE FOUND

Here is the bottom line. Here and now is simply not forever. This world is not the paradise we were designed to live in. As you live in the here and now, the brokenness of this world will collide again and again with the longing hardwired inside you. Yes, sin twists and bends that longing, and it becomes scarily self-absorbed and self-focused. Yes, you will always find ways in which to insert yourself into the center of your world, the one place no human being is supposed to be because it is God's place. You will have times when you moan and complain in your self-absorbed disappointment that life doesn't operate according to your sovereign plan. In your disappointment and anger, you will lash out against the people who live closest to you. You will doubt that the world is under any control whatsoever and fantasize about how much better the world would be if you had the controller in your hands.

Sadly, we all do these things in some way. But with all the ways sin causes us to lose our way, we still get up every day and hook our hope to something. Everything we do is somehow attached to hope. So here is what we need to keep in mind: the brokenness and longing that intersect in our hearts are meant not to drive us to cynicism and despair, but to God. As we begin to realize that in this broken world we cannot look for reliable hope horizontally, we are at the edge of what we were designed to do: hope in God. And as we begin to place our hope in God, we get connected to the promise of eternity, where all that is broken will be fixed and made new again. And as we do this, we look at life in a radically new way. We no longer ask the broken people, places, and things to be the source of our hope. We know they can't be, because they are broken and in need of renewal just like we are.

Horizontal hope will hook us, but it will never fulfill us. Hope that is reliable and will not fail us must have a future. For hope to be trustworthy in the middle where we all live, it must have an end. Hope to be hope must carry with it the promise that all that is broken will be repaired, and that it will remain repaired forever. There is only one place where that promise can be found. To explain why, we must go once again to the garden.

In the garden of Eden, there was no hopelessness. The lives of Adam and Eve were infused with hope. For Adam and Eve, hope wasn't a situation, location, or person. Hope wasn't some dreamy wish for something in the future. Hope wasn't something they would find in the creation. No, hope for them was God himself. God's presence with them, his love and his power, gave them hope. All of the hopes of their entire existence rested on the shoulders of the one who created them. That is where God intended for us to put our hope. Adam and Eve were connected to hope because they were connected to God. And the promise was that as long as they stayed inside God's boundaries, they would live with God in that perfection forever. Now that is hope!

But the horror that never should have been, happened. In a terrible moment of selfishness and rebellion, Adam and Eve willingly stepped beyond God's boundaries and experienced the one thing human beings were never meant to experience: separation from God. They were now estranged from the one who would come and walk with them in the garden and give them that identity, security, meaning, purpose, and inner sense of well-being that every human being seeks. Their world became a world of fear, where discouragement, confusion, danger, and disappointment lived. The shalom of the garden had been shattered, and there was no putting it back together again.

Separated from God, who was to be the source of their hope, Adam and Eve and the generations they birthed began to search for hope horizontally. So we look for hope in the temporary situations, locations, relationships, and possessions of the broken world. We hook ourselves to things that give temporary hope, or no hope at all, going back again and again until we become enslaved and addicted. In searching for hope horizontally, we are shopping for God replacements. But just like wooden idols that cannot see, hear, or speak, these God replacements have no capacity whatsoever to deliver. They quickly leave us empty, always craving for more.

However, as we saw in chapter 4, God was not willing to leave his world in such a sorry state, and so he set in motion a plan that would restore people to God and, in restoring people to God, restore them to a hope that would last forever. As we place our trust in Jesus, we are reconciled to God and are given hope that will never put us to shame!

If you are God's child, you can have hope in the middle of all the tough things you face, not only because in all of those moments God is with you, but also because the cross of Jesus guarantees you that all that is broken will be made new forever. You can live today knowing that you have a future that is beyond the boundaries of your wildest imagination. If you are God's child, you have hope because God *is* hope, and you have a hope that will last forever because he has defeated the one thing that stands between you and forever: death.

Sadly, many of us who by God's grace have been given hope don't live as if we have it. We look for hope where hope can't be found. We place our hope in things that can never deliver. We live hopelessly because we fail to live with forever in view. We live for the next vacation, the next thrilling experience, the next stunning achievement. We put our hope in the hands of flawed and finite people, burdening our relationships with expectations that they can never deliver. We ask inanimate objects to give us a reason to get up in the morning, but they never can.

Sure, the things in which we put our hope give us a temporary buzz and a temporary rest, but reality always hits. These things all disappoint us in the end. No matter how wonderful the situations in our life are, no matter how beautiful our possessions are, no matter how exciting our experiences are, no matter how fulfilling our accomplishments are, and no matter how loving the people in our lives are, they will only satisfy us temporarily. They simply cannot carry our hope. How different would your life and mine be if we remembered that everything that exists in the created world is meant to be a finger pointing us to the only place where hope can be found?

We are often like the five thousand people Jesus fed with a little boy's lunch. They were excited about the physical bread, but they failed to see that that bread was meant to point them to Jesus, the Bread of Life, who alone was able to satisfy the hunger of their hearts (see John 6). When you understand that creation was designed to point to where hope can be found, you don't place your hope in physical things, but in the one who created them and lovingly blesses you with them. What if you were cogently aware every day that looking for hope in the fleeting things of life ends in dissatisfaction, addiction, and ultimately despair? How would your life be different if you lived as though you believed that hope is more than a present fulfillment, that hope, in fact, is a long lens that brings the present into proper focus?

Take a moment and step back and examine your life through the lens of the questions above. In what ways do you ask your relationships, your job, your achievements, or your possessions to give you hope that they will never be able to deliver? How does asking this shape your feelings about these things and your actions toward them? How has looking to these things for hope shaped your relationship with God? Where, specifically, is God calling you to change?

The problem is that it is so easy for us to live as if this life is all there is. It's so easy to forget that on the cross God opened up the doors of forever to all who believe. It is so easy in our eternity amnesia to fall into a frantic daily quest for what has already been given to us in Christ. It is so easy to miss the point that if you are God's child, there is never a moment when you are hopeless. If you are reconciled to God, you are connected to a hope that will extend forever.

Yes, life in a broken world is hard. Yes, we will suffer the reality that we live in brokenness that we often have no power to change. Yes, there are moments when we will feel alienated and small. Yes, we will experience profound disappointment and sadness. Yes, people who we thought loved us will turn their backs and walk away. Yes, there will be nights when the trouble of our life makes it hard for us to sleep. Yes, there will be mornings when we will want to pull the covers over our head and deny the existence of the world. Yes, we will face pain and loss. But if we are God's child, none of these things has the power to negate who we are, what has been promised us, and where we are going. So quit looking for hope where it can't be found and stop asking temporary things to give you permanent hope. Quit burdening people with your well-being. Refuse to shop for what you have already been given. Grace has made you hope rich, so stop living as if you are hope poor.

John, whom you read about earlier, failed to do these things. His assessment of his life was way too here and now. He lived as if there was no reality for him but the present reality. He said he was God's child, that he had placed his trust in him, but he lived as if he were alone and had no future. When Melinda came into his life, John thought that he had found the place where his hope could rest, and without knowing he was doing it, he loaded all his hope onto her shoulders.

In desperation John came to see me. I didn't try to comfort him by telling him I understood or by trying to make him feel better about the tragedy of Melinda's sickness. Instead, I gave eternity back to him. I helped John see, examine, and evaluate life from a much longer lens than the short lens of the here and now. And in giving John back eternity, I gave John a radically different way of understanding and living in the here and now.

John learned to put his and Melinda's suffering into the context of eternity and thus no longer felt bitter. He didn't envy the lives of people who seemed to have what he didn't have. John stopped trying to avoid thinking about Melinda and her sickness. He stopped struggling with the easily irritated impatience of a dissatisfied man. John now approached Melinda and his marriage with a hopeful heart. He had come to know that hope is not to be found in a situation, location, or relationship, but in a person named Jesus. So John was freed from the bitterness and paralysis of his hopelessness. He now was able to approach his relationship with and service to Melinda with a heart at rest. That enabled him to be more attentive and to find more joy in serving her than he had ever had before. He also was freed to run to God in moments when it was hard to do what God had called him to do. John hadn't been running to God for help, because he thought that God had failed him. John began to read his Bible more and pray more, and as he did, his hope grew. John began to live the words that the apostle Paul wrote so many centuries ago: "Therefore we do not lose heart. Though outwardly we are wasting away, yet inwardly we are being renewed day by day. For our light and momentary troubles are achieving for us an eternal glory that far outweighs them all. So we fix our eyes not on what is seen, but on what is unseen, since what is seen is temporary, but what is unseen is eternal" (2 Corinthians 4:16–18).

Is the hope that gets you up in the morning connected to forever?

IS YOUR HOPE CONNECTED TO FOREVER?

I'm going to end this section with a biblical homework assignment: I want to encourage you to study the book of 1 Peter. First Peter is written to people who were suffering. Peter's letter is a practical explanation of where hope can be found and what it looks like to live with hope in a broken world. Chapter 1 roots present hope in the promise of eternity (see vv. 3–9). This chapter also connects present obedience (vv. 13–23) to future hope (vv. 24–25). In the chapters that follow, Peter keeps connecting practical, everyday living to the hope of eternity (see 2:12; 3:9, 21–22; 4:7, 13; 5:4, 10). First Peter 3:15 tells us what this book is about with these words, "Always be prepared to give an answer to everyone who asks you to give the reason for the hope that you have." Here's the scenario that Peter envisions: You're living in a different way than the average person because you have sturdy and reliable hope. A neighbor or friend has observed your living and comes to you and says, "You suffer the same difficulties and disappointments that I do, but you deal with them with hope that I don't have. Where can I get this hope?"

You see, Peter is arguing that we obey (1:13–25), not because God has made our life easy, but because we have eternal hope. We love the thought of being the temple where God dwells (2:1–10), not because God endorses our definition of the good life, but because we have eternal hope. Peter says that we are willing to live here like aliens because we know that this is not our final destination (2:11–12). Peter teaches that we are to submit to the authorities over us and work respectfully in the workplace, not because our bosses are ideal, but because we live in the messiness of the workplace with eternal hope. Peter believes the only way we can deal with the insults of others is when they are not the source of our hope (2:23–25). He teaches that the only way we can have the kind of marriage that God has called us to is if our hope is not held by the hands of our spouse (3:1–7). For Peter eternal hope alone is what enables us to endure present suffering (3:8–22; 4:12–19). Only eternal hope keeps us from functional idolatry— asking things to provide what only God can give (4:1–11). And Peter teaches that the only way we can exercise authority in a way that is not self-oriented and abusive is when we are exercising it, not for our glory, but for the glory of the one with whom we have been chosen to spend eternity.

Take some time to live in 1 Peter. Ask God to let the comfort of its hope change your heart and the call of its hope change the way you live.

Chapter Eight

SUFFERING IS HARDER WHEN YOU HAVE NO FOREVER

I was in Virginia on a ministry trip and awoke to the sound of my cell phone ringing. It was the kind of call no parent ever wants to get. Luella, my wife, was on the other end of the phone, and I was surprised to hear her voice because she is not an early riser. She didn't sound upset as much as concerned as she told me she was heading to the hospital because our daughter had been in some kind of accident. She said she would call again as soon as she knew what was going on.

Her next call had a very different character. She was very upset and told me to get home as fast as I could. The trip home seemed to take forever. Over the course of several more phone calls, I was able to piece together the story of Nicole's accident. It was much more serious than we'd originally thought. Nikki had been walking home from work in Center City, Philadelphia, when a drunk and unlicensed driver lost control of her SUV, careened up onto the sidewalk, and crushed our daughter against a wall. She had massive injuries. We were told later that if this accident had happened in the suburbs, Nicole probably wouldn't have lived long enough to get to the hospital. She had been placed in intensive care after doctors had worked successfully to stop her internal bleeding. The center part of her skeleton had been shattered—eleven breaks of her pelvis along with other injuries.

As I entered my daughter's hospital room that evening and saw her broken body being sustained by machines, I did what any father with even an ounce of love in him would do: I fell apart. I didn't know how responsive Nikki would be, but I couldn't think of anything else to do than to get myself as near to her as I could. I leaned up over the edge of her bed so that my cheek touched hers, and I said, "Nicole, this is Dad. You are not alone. I am with you, and God is with you, and we're not about to leave." As I spoke, tears came coursing down Nicole's cheeks and mine as well.

I have never felt more helpless. I could speak words of comfort to my daughter, but I had no power whatsoever to relieve her suffering. She was in unspeakable pain. Because of the damage to her pelvis, there was no position that was remotely comfortable. She had damage to both legs, and her heart was overworking to compensate for her blood loss. I kept looking at her monitor and thinking that she was going to have a heart attack or stroke. The first three days were very grim. Then on the fourth day, as Nicole was being put through a very painful procedure, the staff overmedicated her and she stopped breathing. I ran down the hall as they were administering oxygen to her. The nurse had yelled for me to come. She wanted me to hold Nicole's hand so she would know I was with her during this moment of intense physical and emotional stress.

The hospital released Nikki after about a month, way too early given the extent of her injuries, so we turned the first floor of our house into a "hospital" for her. I didn't go to work for three months. To make it all worse, we didn't know how permanent or life-changing Nikki's injuries would be. We simply focused on getting her through the day and hoped and prayed that the next day would be better.

From a human standpoint, the timing of this horrible moment in our daughter's life seemed all wrong. She was just beginning her launch as an adult, and in this moment, she lost just about everything. She couldn't think about her work, and most of her friends faded away, not really able to deal with what she was going through. She went through about three years of travail. Her body healed more rapidly than any of us thought it would, but her emotional and spiritual suffering continued for longer than we anticipated. The inner pain was harder for all of us than the physical pain that had initiated it. What none of us knew the day we all headed for the hospital is that Nicole's accident would throw us all into three years of emotional and spiritual travail.

I am thankful to report that Nicole is doing very well today. If you saw her you wouldn't know that she had been through such a significant trauma. She has minor physical issues that she will always carry, but they are insignificant in comparison with the injuries she suffered.

Nicole's accident confronted me with the reality of just how broken our world actually is. It is a world where irresponsible people drive drunk and forever alter the lives of others. It is a world where severe suffering is a daily reality. It is a world where suffering forces us to face how little power we really have. It is a world where an injustice can change the course of your life. We all like to think that with a little planning and responsible living we will be able to avoid the pain others have experienced. But suffering has a way of entering our door, and when it does, we'd better have handholds to reach for that keep us from being swept away by the power, discouragement, and helplessness of it all.

Throughout that three-year period, our family held on to God's grace and the promise that he would give us what we needed to face what were facing (2 Peter 1:3). We held on to the truth of God's sovereignty—our world had not spun out of control, but in ways that were hard to see or understand, it was under God's wise and loving control. And we held on to eternity. No, not just the comfort that someday all of our trials would end, but the peace that comes from knowing that if we are guaranteed a place in eternity, then we can be assured that God will protect and provide for us along the way.

BACK TO THE FUTURE

When suffering enters your door, when you are grieving the loss of someone or something significant, or when you are dealing with unexpected disappointment, where do you look for hope, rest, and comfort? Where do you turn when you are in a situation that you never thought you'd be in and are incapable of altering? What gets you up in the morning when you are being required to deal with things you have no desire to face? Where do you run when people have failed you and God seems impossible to understand? What gets you through when life has quit being easy, regular, or enjoyable?

You may not be suffering right now, but if you aren't, you are near someone who is. What comfort do you offer them? If you are not suffering now, well, you likely will some day. I am persuaded that the deepest of suffering for a human being is not the suffering of physical, relational, or personal loss. No, the hardest part of suffering is the emotional/spiritual suffering we go through as we suffer the loss of those things. It is the pain of not being able to make sense of life, the pain of feeling that God is distant or unknowable, the pain of not having a clue what to do, or the pain of utter powerlessness.

Thus, we don't all suffer the same way. In moments of difficulty, disappointment, and suffering, some of us are tempted to draw wrong conclusions that alter our lives long after the suffering is over. Some of us are tempted to make decisions in the pain of the moment that we later live to regret. Some of us are tempted to break away from those we love and abandon what we believe because life seems dangerous and unfair and we are convinced no one understands or cares. The way you suffer through your moment of difficulty will be shaped by what you brought into that difficulty. None of us comes to our suffering empty-handed; there are response-shaping conclusions about life that will be your handholds when the rug of life appears to have been pulled out from under you.

Forever can radically alter the way we suffer, because it offers us hope and help, not just in the future, but right here, right now. In those dark moments of disappointment and helplessness, as I watched Nicole suffer and had no idea where her story was going, I held on to forever with both hands. Forever offered us much more than some distant future hope, although that hope is a wonderful thing. The promise of forever — the gift of the empty tomb to all who have placed their trust in Jesus — offered us just what we needed when life came crashing down around our feet.

At Nicole's bedside, in our confusion and fear, these are the things that gave us peace, comfort, and courage. The rest of this chapter details what we held on to as we walked through those days that became years with Nicole.

Forever tells us the following things.

OUR LIFE IS NOT OUT OF CONTROL

As I struggled with the difficult circumstances we were facing with Nicole, I was hit with the reality of how little control I have over the things most precious to me. Suffering always confronts us with the fact that our lives do not operate according to our plans. Suffering is almost always unexpected and surprising.

In our suffering, forever reminded us that our life was not out of control but was carefully orchestrated by God, who is powerful, wise, and good. If we carry the truth of forever into our time of difficulty, we will be protected from the panic of thinking that our lives are hopelessly out of control. The future makes all the difference in the here and now.

Think about this: if God hadn't devised an origin-to-destiny plan, and if he had not included you in that plan, there would be no forever and no promise that you would be included in it. Although suffering should confront you with the fact that you do not have the control over your own welfare you thought you had, it does not need to lead you to the conclusion that no one has control over you and your life. Just when nothing seems sure, forever reminds us that before the creation of the world, the God who created and controls all things put a plan in motion, and nothing can thwart his plan. You may feel lost in your circumstances. You may feel that God is not near. You may not be able to figure out why you have been chosen to go through this difficult moment. You may not know how to think properly about or how to respond to what is now going on in your life. But forever tells you that you are not the victim of impersonal forces. Someone is in charge of what is happening in your life. Forever tells us there *is* a God, that he *does* have a plan, that he *is* in control, and that as God's child, you *do* have hope and help because grace has been included in his unalterable plan. This means that as earthshaking as this moment may be for you, your world is not ending and you will not be lost to your circumstances. A place has been prepared for you in the forever that is to come. God is not about to lose you along the way.

But it gets even more radical. If God has written your story and is working out his plan, then your dark moments have meaning and purpose. These moments, which you never would have chosen for yourself, are somehow part of God's plan. His plan clearly is to keep you in this broken world where suffering lives until you are ready for the forever that is to follow. Now, I realize this won't immediately help you understand specifically why you are going through what you are going through, and it won't immediately alleviate your pain, but it will protect you from the fear that God is weak, absent, uncaring, or defeated.

During Nicole's travail, our family held on to the purposefulness of the moment that we were in. We weren't simply dealing with inanimate objects (like the SUV) and impersonal biological forces (in Nikki's body). No, God was working his great plan. If we were dealing only with the forces of fate and biology, we would have had no one to appeal to in our fear and pain, but because the entire situation was in God's good hands, we could run to him again and again and appeal to his mercy.

For reasons that are somehow for my good and God's glory, God has written things into my story that I never would have chosen for myself. Forever reminds me that these things are not so much an argument for God's absence, but a demonstration of his presence. He is working his plan, and part of his plan is to prepare me for what is to come. Just as heat tempers metal, hardship is one of his most efficient tools of personal preparation (see Romans 5:1–5; 2 Corinthians 4:7–18; James 1:2–4; and 1 Peter 1:3–9).

I have told people many times that, if I could, I would choose not to go through again what we endured with Nicole, but at the same time I am very thankful for what I received as a result. I have greater confidence in God's presence and care than I had before. I am more compassionate toward people around me who are suffering than I was before. My pride in my ability to plan and keep my life under control was shattered in a good way. I have learned to pray with meaning the words that Jesus taught us to pray, "Your kingdom come, your will be done on earth as it is in heaven" (Matthew 6:10).

In the middle of our suffering, forever protects us from concluding that God is unfaithful and inattentive. He has made promises to us, and in order to ensure that they will come to be, he is with us and in charge of all the things that seem so terribly out of control.

GOD IS GUARDING US

In our suffering, forever tells us that God has not only guaranteed us a future free of suffering, but has promised to protect us in the meantime. In Peter's first letter, where he puts the forever that is to come and the suffering of this present moment side by side, Peter is writing to people who are suffering. Look at how he connects forever to their suffering:

> Blessed be the God and Father of our Lord Jesus Christ! According to his great mercy, he has caused us to be born again to a living hope through the resurrection of Jesus Christ from the dead, to an inheritance that is imperishable, undefiled, and unfading, kept in heaven for you, who by God's power are being guarded through faith for a salvation ready to be revealed in the last time. In this you rejoice, though now for a little while, if necessary, you have been grieved by various trials. (1:3–6 ESV)

Notice how Peter cannot think about the trouble of the present without looking at it from the perspective of eternity. Notice his language: "living hope," "resurrection of Jesus Christ from the dead," "inheritance ... kept in heaven for you," and "salvation ready to be revealed in the last time." Peter is saying that what is coming is a necessary lens for understanding our present painful experiences. But there is something even more radically encouraging that this essential forever perspective offers us. It is captured by a single word, a word so familiar and so seemingly mundane that your eyes may have skipped right over it without giving it much notice. This little word shows us how the future infuses this painful present moment with help and hope.

The word is found in verse 5, and it is a much more practical word than it is a theological one. The word is *guarded*. It tells us exactly what God is doing in the here and now, and exactly why we can have hope, even in unexpected moments of pain. After telling his suffering readers that they have an inheritance waiting for them in the forever that is to come, Peter says, "who by God's power are being *guarded* through faith for a salvation ready to be revealed in the last time" (emphasis added).

Understand what this one word depicts for you personally. Not only does God have a plan that you are included in, but he is also with you daily and guarding you through every situation as he is preparing you for forever. You see, *guarded* means that not only is your future guaranteed, but it means that God is protecting you in the here and now as well. If forever is in your future, then God must "guard" you between now and whenever forever becomes your permanent address. "Guarded" means you cannot only be assured of future hope, but of the right here, right now comfort of present help.

Let me illustrate this for you. Pretend with me that you have been informed by a local bank that a deceased relative left you a huge inheritance that will be yours to use in the distant future. But then the banker tells you more. He informs you that the person who left the money wanted to be sure that you would be alive and well when the inheritance comes due, so she paid for you to have the care of the world's best physician, dietician, bodyguard, personal trainer, counselor, and financial consultant. He informs you that each of these people is now employed by you and you alone for the sole purpose of guarding your health and vitality so that when it comes time for you to receive what has been promised, you will be there to receive it.

Perhaps as you've been reading you've been thinking, *Paul, God didn't guard you. Look what happened to your daughter.* But *guarded* doesn't mean that God gives me a ticket out of difficulty and pain. No, this promise of protection addresses a deeper danger than the physical and circumstantial difficulties that we all face in this fallen world. *Guarded* doesn't mean that God will protect me from trouble, but rather that God will protect me in the middle of trouble until my troubles are no more. It means that God is with me, and in grace he gives me all I need to face what I am facing with courage and hope. To do this, he gives me all the grace I need to fight bitterness, doubt of God, and the temptation to run away from my faith and give way to panic and fear, bombarding myself with questions no human can answer. These are the regular heart temptations of the sufferer. *Guarded* means that in my moment of suffering, God provides me with protective grace, and because he does, I can have "living hope." This hope is something different than the sterile hope of distant, theological platitudes. It is the security of real provision in desperate times of need.

Every day of your life, whether you have eyes to see it or not, God is guarding you. His presence guarantees that when the door of forever opens, you will be there to walk through it. Not only that, but it guarantees help along the way. The one who promised you forever is your Guard along the way. There is simply no way he will leave your side before you are on the other side with him forever!

WE ARE NOT ALONE

In our suffering, forever encourages us with the reality that God is near. In those days when Nicole's suffering was intense and the doctors had little encouragement to give, it didn't feel as though God was near, so again and again Luella and I would remind one another of the reality of his presence.

I don't want to be unnecessarily repetitive here, but this point bears emphasis: the promise of forever guarantees that in the here and now we are simply never, ever alone! The aloneness of suffering is one of its most painful experiences.

Suffering tends to do two powerful things to us. First, it alienates us from the people nearest to us. It puts a big gulf between us. It makes us feel that there is no way anyone else could ever understand what we are going through. And if they could, they would be just as overwhelmed as we are and be looking for the quickest means of escape. We feel as if we have been swallowed up by suffering, and even though we are in the same room with others, it feels like we are more distant from one another than we have ever been.

Second, the shadow of suffering looms so large, it clouds any sense of God's presence. Suffering is like walking down into a windowless basement on a bright sunny day. The longer we stay in that subterranean darkness, the harder it is to grasp that the sun is still shining. So suffering creates a double alienation. We not only experience the horizontal alienation from friends and family, but we also experience a vertical alienation from God. This is where the promise of forever and its guarantee of God's presence in the here and now are so vital. When our souls are in the darkness, we need to keep telling ourselves again and again that the sun *is* still brightly shining. God *is* with us, even though the present darkness has blinded us from his nearness. We are not, nor will we ever be, alone. The God who has promised us forever has invaded our present so that nothing can get in the way of what he has stored away for us. He is near, and we are not alone.

CHRIST LIVES IN US

The fact that God guards us assures us that we will have grace that is form-fit for our time of suffering. The way God guards his children is not by giving them wisdom and provisions from a distance. He doesn't just grace us with stuff. No, the way God guards, protects, guides, and keeps his children right here, right now, as we wait for the forever that he has promised, is by giving us *himself*!

There is an important distinction to be made here. God not only is *with* us, providing things that we need that we could not provide for ourselves, but he is *in* us, animating us to think, desire, and do things that would be impossible without his empowering presence living inside of us (Ephesians 3:20). God knows this world is so terribly broken and we are so desperately needy that the only thing that will help us is him. So he doesn't just administer our story from a distance; he literally comes to us and lives inside us. He does this so that we will have the grace we need to face what he will call us to face, to do what he has called us to do, and to continue to the end. You see, the promise of forever doesn't just mean that we'll live in his presence *then*, but it means that we are gifted with his presence now.

Think about the radical encouragement of this truth. I may love you, and I may want to assist you in your time of need, but I am always operating from the outside. In your moments of weakness, I cannot get inside of you and give you the strength you need to press on. Yet this is exactly what God does for us. He is with us, providing for our needs, and he is in us with strengthening and transforming grace.

The apostle Paul says it this way in Galatians 2:20: "It is no longer I who live, but Christ who lives in me." Now, Paul isn't announcing his physical death, but is capturing an incredibly encouraging spiritual reality. He is no longer left to the resources of his own righteousness, strength, or wisdom. He is not left to figure out and cope with his circumstances on his own. He does not have to control people and situations in order to establish some kind of inner sense of security and well-being. He doesn't have to be a fortune-teller, reading the future so he can be prepared for what's coming. He doesn't have to look to people and situations to get what only God can give him. No, he is freed from all of those things because of this one stunning reality: *"Christ lives in me."*

This reality has the possibility of radically changing how you think about yourself, your relationships, and the locations where you live and work. It has the possibility of altering the basic way you approach your life. Paul is saying that the life force that now energizes everything he is and does is no longer him, but Christ. Fasten your seat belt here; if you are God's child, Jesus really does live inside you! He comes to you with all the wisdom, strength, and righteousness you could ever need. The Bible has a beautiful name for this: *grace.*

Suffering Is Harder When You Have No Forever

Day after exhausting day of Nicole's recovery, Luella and I were comforted to know that we weren't left to the resources of our own strength as we walked with her through that dark time. When taken beyond the borders of our own strength and wisdom, we had hope because we knew Christ lived inside of us.

Knowing that Christ lives in us makes it possible for us to get up in the morning when circumstances are hard and the relationships around us are messy. We don't have to fear what things we'll have to deal with that are just around the corner. Our rest is not to be found in our understanding of everything in our lives or the sense that we have what it takes to face our trials. Christ is our rest, hope, courage, and motivation. Because of his amazing grace and his presence now living inside us, we are never alone, never left to live inside the boundaries of our own resources.

This truth has significant ramifications on how we live in the here and now, and yet masses of Christians simply do not know who they are or what they have been given. Every day you and I assess our ability to deal with what is on our plate. This personal assessment is an intensely human thing to do. It is what makes a little girl afraid to attempt to ride her new two-wheeler. She has assessed her ability to balance herself on the bike and move forward, and she has determined she is lacking. It is what makes the eighteen-year-old nervous as his parents drive away, having delivered him to his first semester at a university far from home. It is what a future bride does the week of her wedding or a future employee does the night before his first day at work. It is what the patient does who has been diagnosed with a chronic disease. We all constantly assess our abilities, and most of the time we don't realize we are doing it.

If you are a Christian but don't know who you are or what you have been given, you will search frantically for what you already have been given in Christ. You will look horizontally (to people and situations) for what you have already been given vertically. You will live a life of worry, timidity, and avoidance. Much of what you do will be motivated by fear. You will tend to assess your ability by thinking about how big the things are that you are facing and how well you've done in the past. These are not false means of personal assessment, but the problem with them is that, for a Christian, they are woefully inadequate because they do not take into account the radical reality that Paul so clearly proclaims: "Christ lives in me."

Here's the bottom line: forever not only promises us blessing in the future, but it also guarantees us the grace that we need in the here and now. This grace is not a set of things; it is a person, and his name is Jesus! Understanding that God's greatest gift is himself changes the way you live. If Christ lives inside of you, not only is it impossible for you to be alone, but it is also impossible for you to be left to your own resources of character, wisdom, and strength.

WE WILL HAVE LIFE ON THE OTHER SIDE OF SUFFERING

Forever guarantees that we will have life on the other side of our suffering. Our lives won't end as sad songs of suffering, because if we're God's children, we have the guarantee of life after death that will be completely free of suffering. Luella and I worked hard to remind one another not to succumb to the temptation to blow this moment out of proportion. It was hard, but the world was not ending. It was painful, but God had not abandoned us. We tried our best to look through the lens of eternity to see the painful moment we were in and not give it more weight than it actually had.

Now, I know that eternity seems far off. Getting the right perception is difficult, because right now seems big and significant, and the hereafter seems distant and ethereal. Nevertheless, having the right perception is essential, because on this side of eternity, we find it hard to grasp what God says is truly important. Psalm 73:20 characterizes this present life as "a dream when one awakes." In the moment, a dream can seem more real than your true life. But when you wake up, it disappears like steam. The dramatic moment of the dream can't be compared to the many, many years that make up your real life.

What this means is that if you are ever going to properly evaluate your life and properly perceive the suffering you have endured, you must factor in eternity. When you are on the other side, in a place when time is no more and your life will never end, the things that now crush you will seem brief and incidental. Now, don't get me wrong—I am not arguing that this truth makes suffering any less painful in the here and now. I am suggesting that you can only properly value the significance of your trials when you place them up against forever.

Forever tells us that our suffering in the here and now will only be a minute part of our total existence. Since we will live forever, when we add our years in this broken world to the sum total of our existence, they will only make up a microscopic fraction of our lives. We will spend vastly more time in a place where suffering is no more than we have spent where suffering still lives.

Paul captures the importance of this sense of perception in 2 Corinthians 4:16–18: "Therefore we do not lose heart. Though outwardly we are wasting away, yet inwardly we are being renewed day by day. For our light and momentary troubles are achieving for us an eternal glory that far outweighs them all. So we fix our eyes not on what is seen, but on what is unseen. For what is seen is temporary, but what is unseen is eternal."

Notice that Paul does not deny the existence of suffering. He talks about "wasting away" and about our "troubles," but he does so with proper perception in light of eternity. When compared to the forever glory of living with God in a fully restored world, the troubles of today seem light and momentary. If you are God's child, your suffering is not the end of your existence, but a preparation for your final destination. So you no longer allow your mind ("eyes") to be dominated by the struggles of the moment, because you realize that everything that makes up your physical existence in the here and now is passing away. When you see things around you as permanent, they take on too much importance and increase your sense of loss when they are taken away. If you mistakenly think that life is only about who has the biggest pile of possessions and pleasures in the here and now—if you have eternity amnesia—then suffering becomes all the more painful and seems all the more unfair.

The things that suffering challenges, weakens, or takes away, as enduring as they may now seem, *are* temporary. Suffering temporarily robs us of physical and emotional strength. It temporarily robs us of our feeling of closeness to others. It temporarily removes our peace and rest. Suffering temporarily steals our comfort and pleasure. But forever guarantees that all of this *is* temporary. Eternity tells every child of God that the bulk of our existence will be lived in a place of eternal peace, rest, and joy. Life in the hereafter, with all of its perfect beauty, *will be* eternal. From there, today's suffering will look like a light and momentary thing. Forever gives us the right perception.

Sadly, many Christian sufferers cause their own trouble. In the middle of their suffering, they forget who they are and what they have been given. They look at this moment as if it is all there is and all they have. I know, because Luella and I were also tempted to forget that we were the children of the one who controls the present and guarantees our future. We were tempted to forget that we had not been left to the limits of our own resources. We were tempted to view our moment of pain as bigger than it really was. But in our moment of pain, forever was our friend. Eternity not only provided us with future hope, but with living hope in the here and now. So with Nicole we suffered, but not like those who have no future hope.[1]

Chapter Nine

FOREVER AND YOUR RELATIONSHIPS

Amber didn't know it, but she suffered from the same thing many people in her situation suffered from: unrealistic expectations. She didn't really have a bad marriage. She wasn't married to a self-centered, malevolent man. They hadn't lived through loads of difficulty. But Amber was disappointed to the point of being devastated. Her marriage to Jake simply hadn't turned out to be what she thought it would be. They often seemed at odds, didn't seem to have much in common, and spent more time apart than together. Mondays were particularly hard for her because they represented the beginning of "another disappointing week." Often as Jake was getting his stuff together to catch the train into the city, Amber would be languishing in bed, trying to delay the fact that she had to face reality by getting up and going about the work of another week. As she lay in bed, she would not so lovingly look at Jake, wondering why she had decided to get married in the first place. She never thought it would be like this, and she didn't have a clue about how to create the changes that seemed necessary for her marriage to be happy.

Paul looked at his watch. It was 4:30 p.m. on yet another Friday. He had no plans. He dreaded going home to the little house he had purchased in the suburbs, but he couldn't bear going out by himself because that made him feel like a loser. Yes, he had lots of "friends," but they weren't really friends in Paul's sense of the word. To Paul, they all seemed rather self-focused and self-absorbed. He told himself that he could drop out for weeks and not be missed. He wanted something more than golf buddies, and he waited for his friends to want more, but they never showed much interest. In a way, he felt that it was easier to be a loner than to have friends who weren't really friends.

Elisha had maxed out, and she needed to do something about it. Her friends drove her crazy. She was determined to find people she could relate to who didn't have problems. She told someone once that she felt as if she were part of a bad reality show. No, her friends were neither crazy nor medicated, but they always seemed to be dealing with something. Frankly, Elisha dreaded the next phone call and didn't always look forward to Saturday night when they all went out together. Sure they would laugh a lot, but at some point during the evening, someone would lay the latest greatest personal problem on the group. "My friends have too many problems to be interesting anymore," Elisha told herself as she manufactured some excuse that would get her out of the Saturday night gathering.

Amber, Paul, and Elisha are suffering from the same condition. They don't understand where they are living, and so they carry around with them a set of expectations that will only ever lead them to disappointment. But their problems with people are not because of the people that they are with, but because of the unrealistic expectations they bring to those relationships. They bring unrealistic expectations to their friendships because they don't understand where they are living and because the one thing that defines the here and now is not part of their everyday thinking. If there is such a thing as forever—and there is—then this present moment is not forever, and I should not bring the expectations of forever into my here-and-now relationships. Permit me to explain.

Unless we want endless disappointment, we must bring a broken-world, *preparation mentality* to all our relationships. Forever really does define what we will experience in our relationships in the here and now. Amber, Paul, and Elisha have all entered their relationships as eternity amnesiacs, and because they have, they have loaded all their hopes and dreams into the here and now. Day after day they are subtly and not so subtly asking the people in their lives to be what they will never be and to do what they are fundamentally incapable of doing.

Amber, Paul, and Elisha all bring a *destination mentality* to their relationships. Each of them has forgotten that relationships this side of forever are not intended by God to be an end in themselves, but a means to an end. Rather than being the container for our happiness, these relationships are a workroom for the Redeemer to do what he alone can do: change us so we are progressively readier for what is to come. So, as we live through the hardships of change, we can rest assured, knowing that the one who is working on us is protecting us and providing for us at the same time. We can have the security of knowing that in the hardest moments of our lives, our Guardian is with us and will be with us until our hardships are no more.

When we forget eternity, we look to people to give us what only God can give. This always leads to disappointment, frustration, criticism, and conflict. But because we don't see our own eternity amnesia, we are convinced that others are the problem and that they need to change, not us.

This was the case for Amber, Paul, and Elisha. Amber had put all her hopes for the future into her marriage. The things she was experiencing weren't grave marital problems, but things many couples have to work through. But because she had invested all of her hopes and security in her marriage, the problems in their marriage looked to her to be vastly greater than they actually were. Paul wasn't living with the "life doesn't work according to my plan" perspective of eternity, and consequently he existed in the small world of his wants and needs. His eternity amnesia kept him from seeing that rather than his friends being self-absorbed, it was he who was self-focused. The clarifying lens of forever would also have been helpful for Elisha. Her friends were no more flawed than she was. This side of forever, God has chosen for us to live as broken people with broken people, and he uses the messiness of our relationships to transform us by his grace.

Amber, Paul, and Elisha all failed to look at their relationships through the lens of eternity and therefore expected their relationships to deliver things a relationship can never deliver. Each of them forgot that they don't need to look to people for their security and hope because they have a Guardian who will be with them until they are on the other side.

If you asked the average person about the relationship between eternity and a healthy relationship, he or she would probably have little ability to make any practical connection between the two. Yet in my years of counseling many people who were struggling in relationships, I again and again made the connection between eternity amnesia and the difficulties they were facing. In fact, one of the things I almost always did was to *give eternity back to them again*. Below I outline several ways that this essential perspective can bring help and healing to any relationship.

FOREVER REMINDS US OF WHERE WE ARE LIVING

Thousands and thousands of people enter relationships with unrealistic expectations, precisely because they either don't know where they are living or have forgotten. Forever tells us that all relationships exist in a world that is broken and in need of redemption. We therefore need to face the reality that we will not enjoy perfectly happy, regular, predictable, and problem-free relationships.

From the vantage point of forever, a community is a flawed person in a relationship with a flawed person in a fallen world but with a faithful God. Although most of us know intellectually that we live in a broken world and that we live with flawed people, we don't always live in light of what we know to be true. We unrealistically believe that we will be able to experience in the here and now things that will only be our experience in eternity. This does not mean that we should not hope for the best and work for the change and growth of our relationships, but it does mean we should understand the brokenness inside us and in the world around us and how this brokenness impacts our relationships.

Most if not all relationships will go through times of difficulty and stress. A good relationship, then, is a humble and needy relationship in which both parties admit that they haven't arrived and are not perfect. They are approachable, willing to listen to the concerns of the other, willing to admit and face their shortcomings. They do not give way to thinking that they are mature and the other person is not. A good relationship doesn't get stuck in a cycle of expectation, disappointment, criticism, and punishment. It doesn't give way to the hopelessness that often grips relationships when change doesn't seem to be happening. A good relationship is good because each person is patient and understanding. Each seeks to encourage the other to grow while resisting laying unrealistic burdens on the shoulders of the other person.

Amber failed to do these things in her marriage to Jake. She failed to look at her marriage to Jake with the eyes of eternity, and she also failed to respond to Jake with eternity's hope. One of the beautiful messages of eternity is that radical personal heart and life change does happen. All of God's children are in the process of being re-formed. On the other side, we will be radically different people than we once were. So rather than sulking in despondency or giving way to anger and bitterness, Amber needed to turn toward Jake with patience and hope. As I helped her look at her life with Jake from the vantage point of forever, she began to believe that change was possible and that she could be a tool used for his change in God's hands. As Amber lived and responded in hope, she began to change as well.

Keep in mind that there is a difference between a bad relationship and a relationship that has problems. The best of relationships this side of eternity will have problems of some kind. However, a bad relationship is characterized by being *unrealistic* and *unwilling*. Being unrealistic in our expectations of others means that we are consistently asking of them what we would be unable to deliver. Being unwilling means that we frequently call others to changes that we are unwilling to make. Troubled relationships almost always are troubled by unrealistic expectations placed on the shoulders of the other person. If the only thing that will make a person happy is to have a perfect friend or spouse who will never fail him or her in any way, then that person will never be happy! When we demand unrealistic perfection, a kind of living that no sinner on this side of forever will ever pull off, we personalize what is not personal.

Here's an example. Let's say a wife asks her husband to mail a very important item for her on his way home from work. She stresses that this is crucial and tells him she is counting on him. That evening he arrives home, and she asks him if he mailed the item; he sheepishly tells her that he forgot. Immediately she goes on the attack: "I can't believe that you do this stuff to me! I don't ask very much from you! I can't even rely on you to follow through with one little thing! If you really loved me, you would remember the things that I ask you to do for me!"

Should he have remembered? Yes! Should he have followed through? Yes! But let's examine her response. She has personalized what really isn't at its core personal. Her husband didn't drive to work with her mail item and say to himself, "I'm going to drive her crazy today. I won't mail her package—yeah, that will drive her nuts!" Or, "What do I care about her mail needs? If she needs something mailed, she can mail it herself." Now if he had either of these two responses, that would be personal!

What does this story teach us? It reminds us once again that we live in a less than perfect world with less than perfect human beings as our companions. It reinforces that we are going to need loads of patience and grace if we are ever going to live in relationships of love with one another. It reminds us that growth is still needed and possible. It teaches us to hunger for eternity, where we will all be delivered from the brokenness that marks every day on this side. And it teaches us to rest, not in the degree to which the other person follows through, but in the faithfulness of the God who is in us, for us, and with us, and who will not quit working in us until forever is our address.

Our responses to one another are not based on our ability to trust one another, but on the security we have because of our trust in Christ. Not only has he promised to take us out of these problems some day, but he is also with us in them. So when we are confused, hurt, or disappointed, we don't have to close up in fear or come at the other person in anger or look for a way out of the relationship. A Guardian is with us, giving us strength for the moment and enabling us to move toward the other person with honesty, patience, and grace. And when we are looking at a problem from the perspective of the vastness of eternity, we are able to keep it in perspective and to resist turning a garden-variety human weakness into a heinous crime. This enables the other person to be less defensive and more approachable than if we displayed more anger than we should have.

FOREVER TELLS US WHERE OUR HOPE IS FOUND

Sometimes in relationships we are tempted to put our hope, security, peace, identity, and rest in the hands of the other person. This is a dangerous thing to do and never ends in the hope and rest we are seeking. Forever alerts us to the danger of putting our hope in the hands of anything or anyone in this broken world. If you listen to the voices on the other side, as recorded in Revelation (4:11; 5:9–10; 11:17–18; 15:3–4; 19:1–3, 6–8), they will tell you where to find reliable hope. The songs from eternity could be summarized this way: "Lord, we put our hope in you, and you did everything you promised to do."

I have had a thousand husbands and wives say to me, each in his or her own way, "All, I ever wanted was a spouse who would make me happy." Thousands of singles are looking for friendships that will do the same. Each time I hear this, I think, "Well, that other person is cooked!" No human being is capable of holding and protecting anyone else's happiness. No human being can give someone else inner rest. Why? Because every person is broken by sin and in need of the transformation of grace. When we look to someone else to be our place of spiritual wholeness, we place a burden on them that they simply will not be able to bear. Forever reminds us that real rest in a relationship is not to be found horizontally; it is to be found vertically.

What is this rest? It is peace, contentment, and hope of heart that come from confidence in the presence and promises of God. It is not something that we get out of our relationships, but that we bring to our relationships. Rather than relating to someone out of the anxiety of not knowing whether that person will deliver what we are seeking, we can approach that person with the calmness of knowing that God has already given us and will continue to give us what we need. Real rest is to be found in the God of forever, who is wisely and carefully working out his plan. We can trust all of his promises and rest in all of his provisions because he will not quit until eternity is our home.

If we want to build beautiful relationships of mutual trust, we must remind ourselves again and again that each relationship is the coming together of two less than perfect people who together long for eternity, where the difficulties of imperfection will be no more.

FOREVER CALLS US TO PATIENCE AND GRACE IN OUR RELATIONSHIPS

Where you live and with whom you live are not accidents. They are not an interruption. They are not obstacles. The reality that God has chosen for you to live in on this earth is a wise and loving choice. None of it is accidental or divine error. No, it is all divine intention. In our relationships, God calls each of us to wait with patience and with grace.

For example, in the first few years of my marriage to Luella, I wasn't a mature husband. But God was at work in me, and thankfully I am now a different man. In the meantime, God was calling my wife to patience and grace. He calls each of us to wait in our relationships, because the change that is needed is almost always a process.

Remember, God intends the hardships of the brokenness of the here and now to do something good. As you are waiting for eternity, God is using the difficulties of this fallen world to grow and transform you. His primary goal in our relationships is not so much our personal happiness, but personal transformation. Here are two things we all need to know about transformation: first, everyone needs it, and second, it is usually a process.

Eternity calls us to patience and grace in our relationships. These moments of difficulty and disappointment are not a waste. God is progressively transforming us from what we are into what his grace alone can enable us to be. He is rescuing us from ourselves and introducing us to the joys of living for him. He will not waste our suffering, and he will make good use of our disappointment. And in all of this, he is working day by day to prepare us for the eternity that is his gift to all who have placed their trust in him.

So, if we have a forever perspective on our relationships, we will offer others the same patient grace that God offers us daily. He knows we haven't arrived yet. He knows there are times we demand our way or lose our way. He knows there are places where we need to mature and things we need to forsake. But he does not give up on us, and he does not turn his back and walk away. He responds to us with eternity in view, and he will not quit until this time of preparation has given way to the final destination. Forever calls and inspires us to do the same with the people we are in relationship with. A good relationship, whether parent to child, friend to friend, or spouse to spouse, happens when we give to one another the same patience and grace that God gives to us each day.

FOREVER INVITES US NOT TO SETTLE FOR LESS

The problem in most relationships is that we end up settling for less than is our potential as God's children. We learn to make things work that are not working. We learn how to live with things that need to change. We develop the skill of living around our problems rather than solving them. Before long, things that we used to be unwilling to live with become the accepted character of our relationships. We convince ourselves that the way we relate to one another is okay when it's not okay. We all have the ability to argue ourselves into believing that things are better than they really are. We may complain about this or that in a relationship, but we aren't communicating honestly or acting decisively to change what needs to change.

If you are not working to change what needs to change in your relationships, then you are somehow learning to live with the dysfunction. Forever makes it clear that God is not satisfied with the condition we and the world are in. He will not rest as long as his world is under the control of and broken by sin. He is simply unwilling to live with the world and everything in it, including our relationships, not functioning in the way he originally purposed. So he will continue to exercise his power and his grace until everything broken by the fall is completely restored. God calls each of us to the same kind of righteous dissatisfaction—not the kind of dissatisfaction that moans and complains because we are not getting what we want or what we think we need. Not the kind of dissatisfaction that is jealous and envious because we have fallen into thinking that we deserve more than we deserve. And not the kind of dissatisfaction that makes us bitter, critical, and demanding of our spouses because they never seem to match up to our standards for them.

No, God calls us to an eternity-initiated dissatisfaction. Eternity tells us where our story is going and what is possible for us. It calls us to continue to hope, work, and pray until all that God has promised to do in us and through us has been realized. We don't try to make do with less in our relationships when more, much more, has been promised to us. I am saddened when I see people become tired with screaming at one another. Instead of working on themselves and on their relationships, instead of facing their problems and weaknesses with determination and hope, they forge relationships that are more like cold war détentes than true love relationships. Couples navigate their relationships with selfishness and unforgiveness. They stay out of one another's way. They learn what are their taboo topics and nonnegotiable demands. So they're no longer fighting with one another, but the relationships they have don't look at all like what God intended. Their problem is that they have learned to be satisfied with what should deeply dissatisfy them.

Eternity calls us to be dissatisfied until all that sin has broken is fully restored. Eternity lays out the promise of fresh starts and new beginnings; of tomorrows that are not only filled with difficulty, but filled with hope and promise. Your relationship can change! You and the other person can grow. Things between you can be different. Your love can deepen and mature. You can know a unity and understanding that you have not yet known. If you commit to work on your relationship with honesty and approachability, it will be worth it! And God, who is honored by your dissatisfaction and who responds to every one of your cries, will give you a regular and unending supply of grace.

FOREVER REMINDS US THAT IT'S NOT "ALL ABOUT ME"

A relationship in which both parties have inserted themselves into the center of their worlds so that everything is all about them will be one of constant conflict, hurt, discouragement, frustration, and anger. Eternity reminds us that life has not and will not work according to our plan, for the world is moving according to the plan of Another. Eternity humbles us with the inescapable reality that we have been born into a universe that, by its very nature, is a celebration of Another.

Think with me for a moment. What are the celebrations in eternity that are recorded in Scripture all about? They are not about human successes and achievements. They are not celebrations of how people got what they wanted and what they felt they needed. Every celebration of eternity is about one thing: God. Every celebration points to his existence, his victory, and his glory. Eternity reminds us of our place. It reminds us once again that God didn't give us his grace so that we could make our selfish little kingdoms of one work. God did not give us his grace so we could live for our own glory. Eternity reminds us that we were given breath for the glory of Another.

There is no more destructive force in a relationship than self-glory. When I make everything all about me—all about the things I want, the things I feel, and the things I need—I will be endlessly demanding and dissatisfied. When I am in the center of my world, I won't so much love you as I will work to co-opt you into the service of my little kingdom of one. I will be much more concerned about my agenda for you than about God's will for you. I will judge you, not by the laws of God's kingdom, but by the laws of my kingdom. If you help me get what I want, I will be kind to you, but if you get in the way of what I want, I will do what is necessary to get you back in line with the purposes of my kingdom of one.

Sadly, many relationships are a relentless war of human glory, with a constant cycle of selfish demands and bitter punishments.

Eternity can rescue us from ourselves. Eternity reminds us that the one place we must never desire to be is in the center of our world. That is the place for God and God alone. And when God is in his rightful place in our world, we can be in the right place in one another's hearts and forge a unified and loving relationship that is the result of together serving the same King. If you are God's child, you will worship and serve this King forever and ever and ever.

FOREVER DEFINES WHAT LOVE LOOKS LIKE

When it comes to love, we are living in a state of cultural confusion. Many of the definitions and pictures of love that are put before us fall short of what love is and does, so we have no concrete idea of what it actually is. My intention here isn't to give you a definition of love; I have done that in other writing.[1] Here I want to highlight some things that eternity can teach us about the nature of true love. The qualities of love that follow flow out of 1 Corinthians 13, a discussion of love written from a forever perspective (see v. 12).

First, love doesn't quit before the job is done. Love doesn't get mad or discouraged and contemplate bolting in the face of difficulty. You cannot read the Bible's origin-to-destiny story of redemption and not be deeply impressed with God's patience and perseverance. There are places in the Old Testament where it looks as if the world has gone mad, as though all of God's work for and in his people has been for naught. But God does not give up. He will not quit until everything that has been broken is restored. More than anything else, a relationship needs patient and persevering love. This love will produce a kind of hope and help in a relationship that shared perspectives and common interests could never produce.

This will sound harsh, but I think it is true: many relationships are inhabited by quitters. We promise perseverance in difficulty but don't keep the promise. We face discouraging and hurtful moments and tell ourselves that the relationship is over or was never what we thought it was in the first place, and we are on our way out. When we fail to meet one another's expectations, we curse one another with silence, beat one another with words, or shut ourselves off, refusing to be vulnerable and be hurt again. The exposure of all those failings is really a good thing. God is revealing our needs so that we will hunger for new and better. But sadly, often what was God's welcome to something better becomes our reason for quitting. Eternity reminds us that God simply refuses to quit until the job is done. That kind of love is vital to any healthy relationship.

Second, love is willing to suffer. Remember that God paved the pathway to eternity by willingly sacrificing his only Son. If God had been unwilling to suffer, there would have been no hope for us in this life, let alone the one to come! You see, we are tempted to quit because we don't like to suffer. A husband doesn't want to deal with his self-centered and demanding wife who needs to grow and change. A friend doesn't want to have to deal with her distancing and often angry girlfriend who needs to grow and change. Eternity reminds us that we cannot live in close proximity to a sinner and not suffer.

Now don't misunderstand me. Being willing to suffer doesn't mean that I look at a wrong you have done and call it right. Neither does God do that with us. It means that I confront you honestly about the places where you have wronged me, but I do so in a spirit of patience and grace. It means that even though I know you need to change, I do not withhold my love. To treat something wrong as if it were right would not be love.

Eternity calls you to suffer so that change can happen. The fences you build to protect yourself from another's weaknesses are the very fences that keep you from having a relationship of love with them. This does not mean that you should permit an abusive person to continue to abuse you or a selfish person to continue to make unreasonable demands on you. It means that you should look at yourself as being just as needy for God's grace as others are and just as confident of his power to change others as you are of his ability to change you. So you must be willing to step outside of what is comfortable for you in order to be God's tool of change and growth in the lives of others. Eternity teaches us that love always requires that we be willing to suffer for the other's good. Ten million years into eternity, we will still be praising God for his willingness to suffer for our eternal good.

Third, eternity reminds us that true love always forgives. There would be no bright hope of eternity in any of God's people if God was not willing to forgive again and again and again. And he not only forgives, but he blesses us with things that we don't deserve. Forgiveness is one of the principle character qualities of true love. Real love doesn't love only in those times when we are deserving. Real love continues to love when we have no desire or ability to reciprocate. Years into eternity we will still not be able to give God the thanks that is his due, and we will be filled with the sense that we have been showered with forever blessings that we never could have earned. A "you earn it and you'll get it" economy of love will kill any relationship. Eternity humbles us with the reminder that this is just the opposite of what God has given us.

Could it be that you are sabotaging your relationships and don't even know it? Could it be that what your relationships need is a new and healthy dose of eternity? Could it be that your marriage is breaking under the dual burden of self-focus and unrealistic expectations? Could it be that eternity exposes that what you have called love really isn't love after all? If so, you don't have to give way to fear, discouragement, or panic. The God of forever is patient and gracious. Seek his help. He will not turn you away, and he will not rest until his grace has done everything in you that it alone can do and you are like him and with him forever.

Chapter Ten

FOREVER AND PARENTING

Many parents have reduced parenting to a neat system designed to get their kids to do stuff. With the proper set of regulations and corresponding set of punishments, supported by well-placed threats and manipulations, they successfully control the behavior of their children. They call this control "parenting." The problem with this system is that if all parents do is regulate and control their children's behavior, when the children are out of the home and out from under parental control, they will have nothing to guide them. Since their obedience was not formed out of desires of the heart to do what is right, but out of fear of punishment, when they are outside of that system, they will have little internal motivation to obey.

This kind of parenting has no past and no future; it has no orienting big-picture worldview that helps children see that doing what is right makes sense. All it has is this moment. If we coerce our children into serving our will for this moment, we feel successful as parents. So we regulate our children's behavior by threat ("You don't want to know what will happen if I have to come up these stairs one more time!"), manipulation ("You know that mountain bike that you've been looking at? It could be yours. All you have to do is …"), and guilt ("I remember when your father was a happy man"). Because we get short-term responses, we think we are successful, not realizing that our efforts will not yield a long-term harvest of obedience.

But are we really successful parents? Is this actually parenting? Do our kids understand why they should obey? Do they want to obey? Is their behavior motivated by a heart sense of what is good, right, and true? Do the kids see life from the helicopter view, that is, a bigger, grander perspective on things than just the present situation? And does this bigger view of things help them understand themselves, life, God, others, right and wrong, their own motivations and thoughts, and so on? Do they feel any remorse whatsoever when they don't obey? Do they understand why they need authority and why they tend to chafe against it? Are they changing, growing, and morally maturing as human beings? Or are they simply succumbing to the power of someone bigger than them, already dreaming of the day when they will be out from under the constraints they now must submit to even though they don't really want to? When our children are young, we sometimes find it difficult to keep the big picture in view. We are tempted to grab any tool at our disposal to get our children to do what we want them to do. We easily forget that we are called to prepare them to live God's way in God's world.

There really is a much, much better way to parent our children! The Bible is filled with rich perspectives on life that can radically alter the way we think about life and the way we live every day. This book is dedicated to just one of those realities: eternity. Let's consider how the reality of forever can shape the way parents think about parenting.

FOREVER GIVES YOU A REASON TO BE SERIOUS ABOUT PARENTING

Eternity reminds parents that this life is not all there is. It sets before us the truth that this present life is not an ultimate destination for our kids, but a preparation for a final destination. The existence of forever forces parents to acknowledge the inescapable conclusion that life has consequences. Our actions and choices have a greater significance than their present results tell us. The choices we make, the investments we make, and the decisions that we make all have eternal consequences. (More about this later.) We cannot take what the Bible says seriously and buy into the self-centered, pleasure-focused materialism of Western culture that essentially says life is all about play and the person who has the most toys wins. The fact is that life has a plot, and the plot (creation – fall – redemption – destiny) moves all of us toward a destiny. We have to look through the long lens of eternity to understand what God has called us to as parents.

I wonder how many of us are trying to squeeze into an already too busy schedule the task of being God's tool for the formation of our kids' souls. How many of us are too busy pursuing that elusive American dream to have time to invest in the development of our children's hearts? How many of us are sticking our kids somewhere with someone in some kind of activity so we can continue to do the things necessary to achieve the lifestyle of material acquisition and pleasurable experiences that we have named the "good life"? How many of us are trying to squeeze hundred-dollar conversations into dime moments? How many of us are quickly upset when our children misbehave or have a crisis that needs our attention because we don't have the time to respond in a way that would be truly productive for their growth? Are you making time to instill life-transforming perspectives in your children or are you on the fly just doing what works to get them to obey?

How many of us in our irritation personalize the behavior of our children because they are in the way of things we are seeking to accomplish? How many of us are forming a life around this significant calling rather than trying to squeeze it into whatever is left in a schedule that is shaped by the pursuit of some personal dream?

The bottom-line question is this: how many of us parent with eternity in view? Do we view and respond to our children with the radical thought that these little ones are forever beings inescapably marching toward a destiny of some kind? Are we committed to the fact that as parents we cannot live for the moment? We must always have the long view of life in our sights. After all, we have mysteries of the universe to unfold to our children that will alter everything they think about themselves and the world they live in—and one of the most important mysteries is the existence of eternity. How many of us are willing to make personal, career, and familial sacrifices because we grasp the eternal significance of the task that God has called us to?

FOREVER DEFINES YOU AND YOUR KIDS

Forever reminds us that our children were created for something vastly bigger than their happiness or ours. Forever tells us that our children will never exist at the center of their universe. Forever tells us that our children will not write their own stories, nor will we write their stories. Forever reminds us that our children do not belong to us; they belong to God. As parents we are God's agents, commissioned to advance his agenda.

You see, there would be no such thing as eternity if there were not a God who rules over all things and orders the world according to his own wisdom. Eternity forces us to face that we live in a world where we are not the ultimate. We simply cannot overstate the importance of this recognition in the lives of our children. Forever requires us to deal with the reality that we have been born into a world of authority.

As a parent, I cannot do whatever I want to do whenever I want to do it with my children. The authority that I have is representative authority. I am called to represent God in the lives of my children. Forever requires me, as a parent, not just to look outward to define where I want my family to go, but to look upward for my sense of identity, meaning, and purpose.

Why is this important? Because if you are a parent, you have given birth to little self-sovereigns who will want to rule their lives for the purpose of their own self-defined comfort. I never had any of my children say to me, "Dad, if you could exercise clearer authority in my life by giving more rules, I would feel so loved." No, our children again and again fell into thinking that life was all about them and that they were the only authority they needed.

Have you ever seen how babies stiffen their bodies in anger? The cry that accompanies their stiff bodies is not a cry of pain or neediness; it's a cry of anger. If you have made the tragic mistake of getting in the way of what your little one wants, even though that infant is not yet in possession of language, he or she is telling you off. That child is saying, "Oh no you don't! You will not do that to me! I love you and have a wonderful plan for your life! I am the Lord!" Children will again and again insert themselves in the center of their world and make it all about them. They will tell themselves over and over that they are autonomous and self-sufficient. They will demand their own way and will not esteem the authority that God, who rules over all, has placed in their lives. They will think that the happiness of the moment is what is ultimate. So children need to be rescued from themselves again and again. You can rescue your children by introducing to them something vastly bigger than themselves. You will need to introduce them to the ultimate fact of facts, the one fact that gives meaning to every other fact, the fact of the existence, character, and plan of God. They will need to understand God's plot (creation–fall–redemption–destiny) and their place in it, or they will be a danger to themselves. As the parent onsite, you must tell yourself repeatedly that your children do not belong to you. They are forever beings, who by their very nature belong to God. Your children have not been given to you to make your life easier, as if they are your little God-given indentured servants. They do not exist to be props for your reputation or trophies of your success. They are not yours to clone in your image. They are not vehicles to live out your unfulfilled dreams. You must face the profound truth that your children belong to their Creator, and that from their first breath they are marching toward a destiny. This is who God created them to be. Your job is to help them to understand who they are and who God is and what life is all about, so that in the various situations and relationships of their lives they will live in a way that is consistent with God's plot.

Maybe you're thinking, "I don't know how to do this." Well, God has helped you. He has created his world in such a way that the physical things around you point to his existence (see Psalm 19 and Romans 1). He did this so that wherever we look we will be reminded of him and know that, like the rest of creation, we belong to him. For example, I could see God's handiwork one day when I was making bread. I had added yeast, sugar, salt, and some oil to warm water. I was watching the yeast bloom, and I was thinking that this chemical process came out of the mind of God. As I added flour to the mixture, I knew what was going to happen. The yeast would interact with the gluten of the flour, creating a gas, and this plasticine-like substance would begin to expand. And when baked, it would be a light, airy loaf with a crispy crust. Then I realized that there are thousands of chemical physical processes that I depend on and that God created them all. It was a moment of worship for me.

About then, my son came in the door from school. I looked up and said, "Ethan, have you ever thought about yeast?"

"Yeah, Dad," he said, "As I was coming home from school, I was thinking yeast is cool."

"I'm serious," I said, and I went through the process with him. "This is just one of thousands of these processes that came out of the mind of God." And then jokingly I said, "And if God hadn't created yeast, all of life would be a cracker."

He laughed and said, "That's deep."

Reminding your children of the existence of God doesn't mean delivering self-righteous parental sermons at points of disobedience ("You know God is watching, and he could crush you like a bug"). No, it means getting from dough to God and back again a dozen times a day.

FOREVER TELLS YOU YOUR CHILD'S GREATEST NEED

The word *need* can be fuzzy and ill-defined. We use the term loosely. If *need* means "essential for life," then the vast majority of what we say we need we don't actually need. When we misunderstand or wrongly define our needs, we often turn blessings into demands and feel entitled to things that we don't need at all. We never hear our children say, "Dad, I sort of desire — —." Instead, they say, "Dad, I need — —." When your children define something as a "need," they think they are entitled to it, that they have the right to demand it, and that if you love them, you will deliver it.

Parents, it is very important for you to come to grips with the fact that your children will come into the world with a distorted sense of personal need. They will repeatedly turn personal wants and luxuries into "needs," and when they do, they will feel entitled to these things and judge your love by your willingness to provide this thing that they mistakenly think they need. They'll do the same with God.

But something even more significant will happen. Your children will attach their happiness, that is, their inner sense of peace and rest, to the things that they have told themselves they need. They will look to these things to provide them with their identity. They will make it their life purpose to acquire and experience these things. This means that without it ever being a conscious decision, they will look horizontally for things that can only be obtained vertically. They will look to the creation to find things that they were hardwired to get from the Creator. Forever can set them straight.

Destiny reminds us that we are not at the center, and that we are not in control. Our children need to know that the greatest danger in all of life is not to be found outside but inside them. The thing that they need most in life is to be rescued from themselves! Your children need to know that they will never find deep and lasting happiness and rest in chasing some personal definition of need. They need to understand that their hearts' desires will be fulfilled when they find their fulfillment in God.

Your children's deepest need is their need for God; their most dangerous delusion is that they can find life somewhere apart from him. Helping your children daily to "see" God is central to your task as a parent. If you pay attention, you will see your children attaching their inner well-being to something other than God. This provides you the opportunity to not only warn them about the inability of that thing to satisfy the longing of their hearts, but also to point them to God, who can give them the satisfaction of heart they seek.

Our son Justin had just lost his mind. At fifteen, his desires, thoughts, motivations, hopes, and dreams had been captured by a girl. He was looking to her to give him a reason to get up in the morning, to feel good about life, and to have hope for the future—all things no flawed person can give to another person. He would ride the roller coaster of her responses to him. He quit caring about his schoolwork. He quit wanting to be with his other friends. She had become his own personal messiah.

When this kind of thing happens with one of our kids, we have a choice to make as a parent. We can view this as a massive hassle and interruption that we have to deal with, or we can welcome it as a God-given opportunity to help the child see what is going on inside and point him or her to God. We can yell at our child, telling him that he is trashing his life and that he can never see the object of his infatuation again. Or we can begin a conversation with him that helps him understand the danger of seeking from a person or thing what he was hardwired to get from God.

Luella and I began that conversation with Justin. Yes, we told him that he couldn't see this girl for a while, but that's not all we did. We talked and talked. We helped him to see the evidence in his life of what was happening in his heart. When you intervene in this manner, you are giving rescuing grace an opportunity to operate in the heart of your child. Justin began to see the danger in what he was doing, and he is now thankful that we worked in the moment to rescue him from himself.

The God of forever loves our children more than we ever could. In love he will put their struggles in our faces so that we will work to rescue them from danger and point them to him. He won't always do this when it is comfortable for us, but at the moment he knows is best. And in those moments, we will either respond to our children out of hearts that are irritated or hearts that are thankful.

Since God purposefully designed the created world so that everything he made is a visible finger pointing to his glory, it is natural to talk about his existence all the time. It would be positively unnatural not to! For instance, how can you fry an egg without seeing the glory of God? How can you experience a powerful storm without reflecting on God's power? How can you see a mountain, a flower, or a wild animal without thinking about God's creative majesty? Left on their own, children have a perverse ability to look at the physical world around them and not see God. So they need their parents to point them to what is designed to be obvious. The problem is, you cannot point them to what you, too, fail to see.

FOREVER REMINDS YOU THAT THERE ARE CONSEQUENCES

Our culture doesn't like consequences. We live in a "Whatever," "It's all good," "Do your thing," "Pay your money; take your choice" society. We like to think that life is an open game that we play as we want and that there aren't any winners or losers. We like to think we can follow our own path and write our own rules. We like to think that we can do what we want today and somehow avoid tomorrow's consequences. But there is no such thing as planting that doesn't produce some kind of harvest. The same is true when it comes to parenting.

Forever looms before your children to remind them that every thought, word, action, desire, choice, and decision carries with it consequences not only in this life, but in the one to come. Paul says, "God cannot be mocked. A man reaps what he sows" (Galatians 6:7). Things won't always be as they are now. This world is in motion, directed by the unstoppable finger of God toward a final conclusion. A hereafter of reaping will follow the life your children are now living. Forever reminds us that life moves forward; it doesn't go around in circles.

Think of it this way: You have given birth to philosophers, theologians, and archaeologists. Your children may think poorly or improperly, but they never stop thinking. They have a restless desire to figure out what is. They want life to make sense. So they are in a constant conversation with themselves, interpreting their experiences and hoping to make sense out of them. Your children are archaeologists who will dig through the mound of their existence seeking to understand their own history. So to impart to them a theology of consequences is very important.

A theology of consequences is not the same as an abstract appreciation of some impersonal law of cause and effect. The existence of eternity forces you to the conclusion that the world in which your children live is a world under careful and constant rule. The God who created and rules all that is, is working his plot. The will of God will be done. He has not only created life as your children know it, but has also designed how it is to be lived. Since they were created for him, designed to live with him in view, and hardwired in the beginning to live with him forever, consequences must be thought of vertically and relationally. Disobedience is not first about the breaking of some abstract rule; it is about breaking relationship with God. When your children ignore God, they find it easy to disobey his commands. Consequences have to do with the authority of God and the ultimate question of whether your kids have lived in submission to his will in the particular relationships and situations that make up their lives. Imparting to your children a *harvest mentality* is a very important piece of what it means to function as God's agent in their lives. So we need to talk to our children repeatedly about the loving heavenly Father who graces us with his wisdom and sets up for us boundaries of protection, which don't rob us of life, but offer us life as it was designed to be enjoyed.

FOREVER CALLS YOU TO PROCESS PARENTING

Children have a shortsighted approach to life and live for the moment. They are ruled by this moment's thought, this moment's desire, this moment's emotion, this moment's dream, or this moment's crisis. They don't take the long view of things, let alone look at life from the perspective of eternity. So it is important that their parents introduce them to *long living*. To do this, you must remember what viewing life from the vantage point of eternity tells you about life in the here and now.

Forever calls you to think of life as a carefully administered process overseen by a God who is wise, loving, and good. He calls us to follow him, making his process of preparation (change and growth) our personal agenda. In this way, every event in our life has meaning and purpose, but no event is ultimate. Each situation is an occasion of and an opportunity for growth.

So how do you keep God's process in view as a parent? First, you tell yourself that whenever your eyes see or your ears hear of the sins, weaknesses, or failures of your children, you are never to see them as interruptions or hassles. These moments must always be viewed as times to show grace. God loves our children. He has put them in a family of faith, and he is giving us opportunities to be part of his loving process of rescue, change, and growth.

Second, you must be willing to lovingly repeat yourself over and over again. Since change is almost always a process, we can't expect to have one encounter with one of our children that will forever change that child. Rather, we need to be committed to many mini moments of change.

Third, we are not called just to announce failure and enforce consequences, but to be God's instruments of heart change in our children. So, in moments of correction, we must always be asking, "What does God want my child to see that she is not now seeing, and how can I help my child see it?" To commit to change in our children, we need to see where change is needed. You see, our children cannot grieve what they do not see, and they cannot confess what they do not grieve, and they cannot desire to change what they have not confessed. Process parenting means finding joy in doing these things again and again.

As parents we have to know where we are going with our children. We always have to have the goals of heart change and life change before our eyes. We have to resist being emotionally reactive and see each new moment of instruction, correction, encouragement, or discipline as a God-given opportunity to take one more step toward our goal. And we can't try to accomplish in one moment what will only happen by means of a process. We must wake up every morning with a process mentality, thankful and expectant, knowing that we will again have opportunities to gain ground toward our goals.

As you take the long view of things, resisting treating this moment as isolated or ultimate, you teach your children to do the same, having conversation after conversation that requires them to think of their lives in vastly bigger terms than the needs, feelings, and wants of the moment.

Many parents fall into the habit of talking *at* their children instead of talking *with* them. To talk with them, you have to be willing to forsake the spontaneous lectures so tempting to every parent and commit yourself to asking and listening. Our goal is not only to have a conversation, but to have one that stimulates accuracy of self-view and a hunger for God's help. I have found a series of five questions to be very helpful in stimulating this kind of conversation.

1. *What was going on?* Here you are getting your child to give you a summary of what happened in the situation you are about to discuss.
2. *What were you thinking and feeling as it was happening?* This helps your child to think about how his heart was interacting with whatever was going on.
3. *What did you do in response?* With this question you are helping your child to see that his behavior was not shaped by the situation, but by how his heart interacted with it.
4. *Why did you do it; what were you trying to accomplish?* Here you are helping the child to examine his motives. He did what he did because he was after something.
5. *What was the result?* This question enables your child to see the connection between his desires, behavior, and the consequences he is now dealing with.

Remember, the purpose of these questions is not to indict a child for some wrong, but to help him see things about himself that he wouldn't otherwise see and to reach out for the help that only God can give.

REST IN GRACE

The more we view life from the perspective of forever, the more grace-oriented we will be as parents, because the forever story of Scripture is a grace story.

In the long process of parenting, we won't always have everything figured out. We won't always feel capable, knowledgeable, and wise. We won't always feel loving toward our children. We won't always feel strong and prepared. We won't always say and do the best thing. We will have days when parenting seems burdensome and discouraging, and we will have moments when we feel like quitting. We will have times when we feel that we're constantly playing catch up—just when we think we understand our children, they will move on to another stage in their development.

As parents, we will never be able to rest in our knowledge, character, or skill. If anything, being a parent will expose our weaknesses in a way that few things expose them. That is why real rest is found only in a deep-seated belief in the resources of grace that are yours in the daily presence of a Redeemer who has come into your life and is working his eternal plan.

Saying that you get the values, motivations, and encouragements you need to be a wise and faithful parent only when you view this important task from the vantage point of eternity is not an overstatement. From this perspective we will be reminded of how important our task is and how blessed we are to be the recipients of an eternal grace that meets us in our weakness and takes us where only grace could enable us to go. And we can get up every morning, not knowing what we will face, but assured that forgiving, empowering, delivering grace will be with us until forever is our final address.

I will close this chapter by telling you how that grace once met and changed me. What seemed like just another weekend in the life of a parent of a teenager proved to be so much more. Our son had asked us if he could spend the weekend with a friend. We knew the family and were glad to say yes. What we didn't know was that he was not spending the weekend with his friend. He had asked his friend to cover for him so he could go somewhere he knew we would not allow.

On Saturday afternoon I got a call from the friend's mother, informing me that our son was not at her home. Her son had begun to feel guilty and had confessed to his mom, and she had made the difficult phone call to us. I got off the phone and was livid. I couldn't believe that our son would look me in the face and lie to me. In anger I stormed upstairs and blurted out to my wife, "Guess where our son is this weekend?" and I told her the story of his deception. Luella could feel my anger, and she said, "I think you need to pray." I said, "I don't think I can pray for him right now." She said, "I didn't mean for you to pray for him; I think you need to pray for you."

I went to my bedroom to pray for God's help, and it hit me that, because of his love, God had already begun a work of rescue in my son's life. God was the one who pressed in on the conscience of my son's friend, causing him to confess to his mom. God was the one who gave her the courage to make that difficult call to me. (I was her pastor.) And God was the one who now was giving me time to get ahold of myself before my son came home. Now, rather than wanting to rip into my son, I wanted to be part of what this God of grace was doing in this moment of rebellion, deception, hurt, and disappointment.

When my son got home on Sunday afternoon, I didn't pounce on him at the door. I let him relax for a couple hours and then went down to his room. I knocked on the door and asked him if we could talk.

"Sure," he said, so I asked him to turn down his stereo.

"Do you ever think about how much God loves you?"

He looked at me a bit confused and said, "Sometimes."

"Do you ever think about how much God's grace operates in your life every day?"

He looked up at me but didn't speak.

"Do you know how much God's grace was working in your life even this weekend?"

He looked up at me with concern on his face and said, "Who told you?"

"You have lived your life in the light. You've made good choices. You've been an easy son to parent, but this weekend you took a step toward the darkness. You can live in the darkness if you want. You can learn to lie and deceive. You can use your friends as your cover.

Forever and Parenting

You can develop the skill of creating a good backstory. You can step over God's boundaries. Or you can determine to live in God's light. I'm pleading with you: don't live in the darkness; live in the light." Then I said, "That's all I want to say to you right now. I love you."

As I turned to walk away, I heard his voice from behind me saying, "Dad, don't go." And as I turned around, with tears in his eyes, he said, "Dad, I want to live in the light, but it is so hard. Will you help me?"

And we began a much lengthier conversation.

If God in grace hadn't caused me to discover my son's deception in time to get my heart where it needed to be, that moment of transforming grace between my son and me would not have happened. I would have found out later, gotten in his face, ripped him apart with words, and walked away. I would have called it Christian parenting, but it would have been neither Christian nor parenting. It would have been an explosion of self-righteous parental anger that would have left the heart of my son utterly unchanged.

You see, eternity doesn't just offer you the future grace of a forever free from the trials you daily face raising flawed children in a fallen world. Eternity offers you the promise of present grace. That grace comes in the faithful presence and provisions of your Redeemer. It's the gift of grace upon grace upon grace until forever is your final home. This grace gives you everything you need so that you can be an instrument of heart- and life-changing grace to your children. You don't have to try to do by the force of your anger, by the threat of a harsh punishment, or by the power of your words what only grace can do. If you and I had the power to change our children, God's grace wouldn't be necessary.

Parent, if you are God's child, forever is not just your future; it is your guarantee of grace in the here and now. That grace meets you in your toughest moments and works to change you so that you can be God's tool of change in the hearts of your children. And that grace is with you and will not wear out before eternity is your reality.

Chapter Eleven

FOREVER AND YOUR JOB

Chad didn't hate his job; it was work that drove him crazy. He forced himself to get up in the morning, trudged his way through his workday, and counted the minutes until he was in his car and heading toward home. His house was a picture of how much he hated work. His garage was so full of debris that he could no longer get the door open, let alone park his car in it. His decaying house, in need of minor repair jobs that had been left undone for too long, was a testament to his distaste for labor.

Chad had had a string of short jobs. The story would go like this. He would get to the place where he couldn't stand his work, begin to look for another job, get interested in a new position, quit his old job, and begin to work at the new place, begin to hate the new job, and repeat the cycle again. He had worked at so many places because he thought the particular job of the moment was the problem, but it wasn't. Chad's view of work was the problem, so no matter where he worked, he always ended up hating it. The long cycle of short jobs didn't advance his career, and it wreaked havoc on his finances.

Chad lived for the weekends; it was when he came alive. He said the weekend was the only thing that helped him to get through the week. He met his wife, Maria, on one of those weekends. When they were engaged, she was excited at the prospect of spending her life with a guy who seemed to be so alive. But after seven years of marriage, she was no longer excited. She hated how sullen Chad was throughout the week and how much he complained about his job. And she was discouraged that he didn't seem to care about how his job changes had hurt their finances.

Chad spent more on play than he did on Maria or their children. She hated that he was always able to find money for another one of his toys. It made her angry that the house was in disrepair but all of Chad's toys were kept in fine working order. She resented each new expenditure and couldn't believe she had allowed herself to marry such a selfish man.

But Chad's absence hurt her even more. Maria was tired of being a weekend widow. Chad's list of activities seemed endless — golfing, fishing, hunting, four-wheeling, jet-skiing, snowmobiling, playing softball and basketball on leagues, and using his season tickets to attend hockey matches. Maria was seldom considered and almost never included. Chad seemed obsessed, as if he feared that his time would run out before he had experienced all the pleasures on his list. On the few occasions when his weekend activities were canceled, he stayed home pouting. In his view, work was a curse — the nasty price you paid to be able to pursue and afford the pleasure that life is really all about. Chad saw little reason for or dignity in work, and he was constantly jealous of the "rich guys" who had gotten to a place where they didn't have to work anymore. Chad was headed for disaster. He was destroying his career and his marriage, and he didn't seem to know it.

Samantha was headed for disaster for the same reason, although it manifested itself quite differently. Samantha was the classic workaholic. She couldn't work enough. She worked long hours at the firm that she had been with for five years, and she ran an interior decorating business out of her home. Samantha loved the next challenge work would give her. She loved the competition for the next rung on the corporate ladder. She loved stepping into problems and working toward a solution. She loved the fact that she had people working for her who were hired for the sole purpose of expediting her orders and realizing her vision. She loved the accolades and power that work gave her. Samantha was never satisfied. Each accomplishment made her hunger for the next. She never seemed to have enough money or power. She never felt too busy or stressed. She loved the frenetic pace, and when she was away from work, she was quickly bored.

Samantha's boyfriend, Ethan, like the others before him, was bothered that Samantha never seemed to get away from work. Oh, he would finally guilt her into taking a day off, but she would be on the phone constantly and would refuse to go anywhere or do anything that would not allow her iPad to be near. Ethan spent many of those days "together" alone as Samantha yelled at an incompetent employee or sealed the next big deal, phone in hand, doing what she loved the most. Whenever Ethan would complain, Samantha would say, "Ethan, I'm investing in the future; it would be good if you would too." But that wasn't the real reason she worked so much. No, Samantha worked because she was hooked on work. She loved work. It was both what she lived for and what made her feel alive. If it weren't for her business at home, the weekends would have driven Samantha crazy. When Samantha was home, she really wasn't "at home."

Ethan was tired of having a girlfriend but spending most of his time alone. He was tired of every conversation he had with Samantha being dominated by work. He had fantasies of grabbing her cell phone and throwing it as far as he could. He was mad that he spent so many evenings alone, and he dreaded the thought of Samantha getting yet another promotion and more responsibility. Meanwhile Samantha was dissatisfied with her present position and working harder and working longer hours than she ever had in hopes of getting the spot she now had her eyes on. She was headed for disaster and didn't even know it. Ethan would soon tell her that he wouldn't compete with her job anymore. For all her success, Samantha would be alone once again.

On the surface, it looks as though Chad and Samantha exist on opposite poles of the universe. It seems as if they share nothing in common, but actually they are suffering from the same thing—eternity amnesia. They don't get the plot of the story, and because they don't, their work life is out of whack. For Chad pleasure is all there is and work is a curse. He is working hard at packing all the pleasure into his life that he has time for and can afford. For Samantha work is all there is and free time is a burden. She is working hard at packing in all the achievements that she has time and strength for. Both are treating the present as if it is all there is.

TWO SIDES OF THE WORK STRUGGLE: ADDICTION AND DISAPPOINTMENT

Today someone will face a crushing disappointment at work. Perhaps the promotion she has been working toward for years will be given to someone else. Or maybe he will receive a poor review on his quarterly evaluation. Maybe her boss will go back on a promise or a fellow worker will prove to be disloyal. Or maybe he will be told that his services are no longer needed, even though he has given himself to the firm for years. In moments like this, it is important to have work in its proper place. Looking at your work from the perspective of eternity is vital. Your work is not the final word on who you are, and it surely should not define what your life is all about. When you view your work from eternity, you remember that your work is your calling, but it is not your life; you remember that work gives you dignity, but it is not your hope; and although you work with diligence, you understand that this place of work is not your final destination, but a preparation for the eternal destination that is your final home.

So when your boss is unfaithful, your coworkers are disloyal, or your job ends, you are disappointed but not crushed. And in your disappointment, your heart longs to be in that place where you continue to work, but your work will be free from the thorns, thistles, suffering, frustration, and disappointments of the fall.

Today someone somewhere is becoming more and more addicted to his work. The power, position, and achievements of career are becoming the drugs that get him through the day. He is investing more and staying longer, and as he does, important things in his life are beginning to suffer. No longer is his relationship with his wife and family central to what makes him tick. No longer is his relationship with God the central motivation of his heart. Instead, work has risen in value until it has become the thing that defines him, and it now functions in his heart in a way that only God should. Work has become his life-giver, his own personal messiah, yet he doesn't know it has happened. He is about to bring trouble to or destroy valuable things in his life as he takes another hit of the power and position drugs that work provides.

It is here that the reality of eternity provides rescue. Eternity rescues us from ourselves and our tendency to assign value to things that are not nearly as valuable as we have made them out to be. It is here that we need to listen to the voices from the other side that are recorded in Scripture and remember who we are and who God is and the greater glory for which we were designed to live.

Disappointment and addiction both are signs of eternity amnesia. Perhaps someone has forgotten the plot of God's story, and therefore physical things have become more important than spiritual things. If so, hope and help are available. God meets us in our addiction and disappointment. His grace opens our eyes and protects our hearts. His grace helps us to see what is eternal and to love what is valuable, and in so doing, once again rescues us from ourselves.

But there is more. Think about it with me. Both Chad and Samantha are in a frantic search for life: real, satisfying, fulfilling, heart-engaging life. Both are on the same driven quest. Why? Because this hunger was hardwired inside them by their Creator. But the tragedy is that both of them are looking for life where it can't be found. Do you remember the eternity plot—creation–fall–redemption–destiny? God created a forever world, but because of an act of rebellion against his authority, sin entered the world and death with it. That means that every physical thing in this world is passing away. Chad's toys and Samantha's work are passing away. Chad's pleasures and Samantha's achievements are passing away. Living for something that is in the process of dying makes no sense, yet that is exactly what Chad and Samantha are doing. There is nothing wrong with enjoying pleasure and nothing immoral about working hard. But when your work or your pleasure have risen in importance until they have become your replacement messiah, then something is terribly wrong with the way you are living.

You see, physical work and physical pleasure are brought into proper balance only when they are viewed from the perspective of eternity. Let's consider some things that eternity teaches us about work and pleasure.

PLEASURE IS NOT THE KEY TO HAPPINESS

The balance of work and pleasure is delicate and tricky, and both the slackers and the workaholics get it wrong. Pleasure is pleasurable because God created pleasure to be pleasurable. Work *is* fulfilling. Pleasure *is* enjoyable. Both are legitimate aspects of God's creative artistry and legitimate pursuits of humanity. Imbalance happens when we look to either for that deep and abiding peace and rest that every human being seeks.

Now let me be clear. Chad and Samantha are actually after the very same thing: pleasure. Chad gets his pleasure through his toys, and Samantha gets her pleasure from her work. And it is not wrong for them to find joy in work or play. The problem comes from what they are asking work and play to do. Both have the same mistaken theology that life is found in the pursuit of the experiences and pleasures of this physical world. I doubt that Chad and Samantha have thought about the way they are living with the clarity of what I have just stated, but this is what they are doing. They are asking this temporary and physical world to give them what it cannot possibly give them: life.

Scripture reminds us of the impermanence of this physical world, warning us that these temporary things have no capacity to satisfy the deep longings of our hearts (see Matthew 6:19–33; Luke 21:33; 2 Corinthians 4:16–18). No wonder Chad and Samantha are driven. No wonder they are dissatisfied. They are looking for life where it cannot be found.

Eternity tells us where life is to be found: in Jesus Christ. What is the hope of eternity? Life with God forever. What is the horror of eternity? Separation from God forever. If you get the plot, you realize life can never be found horizontally. Eternity is a beautiful hope, because for all who have placed their trust in Jesus Christ, he will be there! The life he gives isn't temporary. He is eternal. His Word is eternal. His promises are eternal. The hope he gives is eternal. The love he bestows is eternal. His presence is eternal.

So if we live in light of eternity, we know that life cannot be found in the temporary pleasures, possessions, and achievements of this world that is passing away. We start investing in eternal life right here, right now. Our life is ruled by a life-shaping pursuit of God. This means we take seriously anything in our lives that connects us to God, his presence, promises, and provisions. For instance, you attend your small group, not because you have been guilted into doing so, but because the fellowship there reminds you of the most important thing in your life, your relationship with God. You look forward to your weekly worship service because it again and again rescues you from the delusion that life is all about present pleasures. You contribute money to Christian ministries, not just to invest in what is eternal, but because it reminds you of what is important and lasting. You read your Bible each morning, not to prove you're a good Christian, but to start your day by reminding yourself of where life is to be found. And you don't keep investing in bigger and better, because you know the message of eternity is that only God can satisfy your heart. You don't let yourself take for granted the many evidences of God's goodness and grace in your life. You cannot be thankful without remembering the Person who gave you the things you are grateful for.

As I described above, living with eternity in view means living with God in view. Our hunger for life is a hunger for God that he hardwired in us when he made us. If the glorious hope of eternity is *him*, then it makes sense that life right here, right now is found only in living with him in view—that is, looking to him for life.

WORK IS NOT A CURSE

Many people have a distorted view of work. They think that work is a pain; or even more destructive, they think that work is a curse. The thinking goes this way: when Adam and Eve fell, part of their punishment was work. But that is a misunderstanding of the biblical story. Adam and Eve were not punished with work; their punishment was that their work would now be hard and toilsome. The fallen state of the world would make their work hard in a way it had never been before.

Adam and Eve were designed for work, and they were commissioned by God to work before sin and death had ever entered the world. As creatures made in God's image, Adam and Eve were commissioned by God to use their wisdom, creativity, and strength to dress and maintain the garden where God had placed them. Their ability to work and their commission from God to work were expressions of their unique position in creation and their dignity as creatures made in his image.

What does this have to do with forever? Well, if God's purpose in eternity is to restore all that sin has broken, then work will be restored in eternity's new heaven and new earth. Work is not so much a consequence of sin as it is an aspect of our humanity. Therefore, in eternity we will work forever.

So to work with eternity in view means to forsake a "grin and bear it" view of work. To work with eternity in view means to work with perseverance and joy, knowing that in work you express the dignity of your position as a being made in God's image. But there is more. This eternal view elevates work from being a necessary but painful means to being an end—working in order to enjoy the pleasures that work can buy. Work has value in and of itself.

In our work, we point to the beauty of God's design and to the wisdom of his plan. In this way, our work becomes one of the chief ways that we live for and point to God's glory. And the reality of eternity reminds us that work is not just something we do in this fallen world. No, work is part of who we are, human beings made in God's image, and God's plan is that we would work to his glory forever.

Neither Chad nor Samantha had any larger glory in mind for their work than their own glory. For Chad, work was the painful price for his play; and for Samantha, work had no bigger purpose than the glory of her own achievements. And blind to the reality of eternity, their work became something that it was never designed to be.

NEITHER OUR WORK NOR OUR PLAY BELONG TO US

People often think that this life of work belongs to them. In this view, the why and how of our work are entirely up to us. However, the existence of eternity, with its creation-fall-redemption-destiny plotline, puts God smack-dab in the center of the universe he created and sustains. Since the universe moves according to God's command and for his glory, we will never be the center.

Living in light of eternity means living with a constant and practical God focus. It means asking what God's purpose and will are for every area of our lives. It means caring about a greater glory than our own and living for a bigger pleasure than our own. It means recognizing that nothing in our lives really belongs to us. All of the physical, emotional, volitional, and conceptual faculties we exercise at work belong to the Lord and are meant to be used in a way that pleases him. Eternity reminds us that we have been born into a world that by its nature is a celebration of another.

From eternity's perspective, we are neither the owners nor the bosses of our work lives. God controls our gifts, our location, our opportunities, the obstacles that we will face, and the success or failure of our labor. It is only when we recognize his existence and his unstoppable plan that we are able to be industrious in our work without being driven, and restful without being lazy. Because we won't just focus our eyes on the things that are passing away (physical pleasures and achievements), we will care more about and be motivated by things of eternal significance (the presence of God and our relationship to him).

WHAT IS IMPORTANT IN OUR WORK IN THE HERE AND NOW

All of us face this problem: staying alert to what is really important in life. Every day you and I must decide again and again what is important and what is not. When things become more important to us than they really are, they shape how we think about ourselves and how we live our lives.

Think about how relatively unimportant things can capture our emotions and set the agenda for our responses. Let's say you are single and living with two housemates. As you are walking out the door of your condo, you notice that your TV room could use a little accent rug. So, on the way home from work, you pick up a nice cream-colored shag rug that is perfect for the space. The next morning you are the last to leave the house, and as you are turning off the lights in the TV room, you notice that the rug you bought has a big red stain on it. In a second, you make a judgment as to how important that rug is. If you judge it to be important, you are immediately filled with rage and are thinking about which one of your housemates you're going to yell at first.

What is happening here? The rug is a collection of threads sewn together, but it commands your emotions and sets the agenda for how you are going to respond to important people in your life. This side of forever, it is hard to keep what God says is important, important in your life.

Many people are confused about what is important when it comes to work. A job or career can rise in importance until it becomes the thing that gives us identity and purpose. If our jobs become too important, we will let them define us more than they should, and we will allow ourselves to work more than we should. And since we have limited lives, our jobs will take time, energy, and motivation away from other more important things, causing them to suffer as a result.

The celebrations in eternity that are recorded in Scripture are not about human position, power, or achievement. They are about God's position, God's power, God's faithfulness, and God's grace. They celebrate God's victory over evil and the eternal life God gives us. These celebrations remind us of what is essential and truly important, and they welcome us to live in light of these values today.

In Luke 12:15–21, Jesus tells the story of a rich man whose values were all wrong. His life was all about accumulating wealth in the here and now. He worked so hard that he produced more crops than his barns could hold. Instead of accepting that overflow as a warning sign that maybe his values were wrong, he tore down his barns and built bigger ones. He lived as if there was nothing more to life than working hard and accumulating wealth. He looked at his big barns and essentially told himself he had it made. As successful as he looked, Jesus called that man a fool, because he lived without any recognition that his life would soon end. Jesus then said that anyone is a fool who lays up riches on earth but is not rich toward God.

In a world that idolizes power, position, fame, and material wealth, we constantly need our sense of what is important clarified and reoriented. The celebrations of eternity provide for us a check of our internal importance meter and call us to live and work in light of what is truly eternally important. They remind us not to let things that are meant to point to Jesus become the things that replace Jesus in the here and now.

FIXING OUR EYES ON WHAT WE CAN'T SEE

We must understand two things to have the proper perspective on the place of work in our lives. First, we have been created with two vision systems. While our physical eyes allow us to see the physical world that God has designed for us to live in, we also have another vision capability—the eyes of our hearts. When Paul says in 2 Corinthians 4:18 that he looks to things that are unseen, he cannot be talking about his physical eyes, for physical eyes have no ability to see the invisible. Paul is talking about "seeing" things that are real but are unseen. If you are ever going to be what God created you to be and do what God designed you to do, you must constantly be alert to the world of spiritual realities. You must "see" God's presence. You must "see" the resources of his grace. You must "see" your deep need of him. You must "see" the truths that he has revealed in his Word. You must "see" the reality of eternity. When you "see" these things, you acknowledge their existence and can then live in light of them.

Maybe you're thinking, "But in the busyness of my life, I go days without seeing these things." Let me suggest something that may help correct your vision. Begin each day by praying that God would give you the eyes to see the spiritual realities that are beneath the physical things that keep you so busy. And then determine to open your "eyes." For example, beneath all of those little skirmishes we have with our children as we try to parent them is a spiritual war that we need to see. There really is a battle for their hearts, and when we "see" it, we parent with endurance and grace. In the middle of our quest for a promotion at work, we must see the reality of the God who has promised to provide for us. We need to see that beneath that disappointing situation with a friend is a relationship with a Savior who will never be disloyal or turn his back on us. In the middle of our confusion about where our lives are going, we need to see a God of wisdom and power who is moving our stories along. Pray for "eyes" to see and require yourself to take another look.

We must also understand that the physical things our physical eyes see are all impermanent. Everything our eyes are now looking at is in the process of passing away. So if the eyes of our hearts are blind, and all we see are the physical realities around us right here, right now, then we will live for those things. But if our eyes are not focused on the physical, and by grace we are able to see what is spiritual, then we can live for things that are eternal.

As we work our physical jobs, we don't just focus our eyes on all the physical locations, situations, relationships, and material things of our work, but we look at what is unseen as well by working with a consciousness of God's presence and remembering his grace. We see our place in the work of God's kingdom. We work conscious of the way he has called us to live. We work thinking about his power and his glory. We work remembering that this moment is not all there is, that there is an eternity to come. And in this way, the unseen world of spiritual realities sets the agenda for how we live in and respond to the world of physical realities that is our address for this moment. When we do this, we are living and working with things of eternal significance in view and are protecting ourselves from a dangerous now-ism that allows us to be all too addicted to what is temporary.

I am thankful that Chad and Samantha reached out for help. The curse that was messing up Chad's life wasn't the curse of work, but the curse of his distorted view of work. I helped him to see that work was such an essential part of God's design for him—and therefore an inescapable part of his identity as a creature made in God's image—that he would be working when forever was his final home. I told Chad that treating work as a curse was like treating breathing, eating, seeing, or hearing as a curse. He had to begin to believe that work was not God's punishment of him, but God's plan for him; that work was part of the perfect world before the fall, part of life in this broken world, and would be part of his destiny in the restored perfection of eternity. I helped Chad see the beauty of work: the natural gifts that were expressed as he worked, the wonderful things that God used work to provide, the character that faithful work builds, the dependency on God that endurance in work encourages, and the longing for forever that work in the fallen world creates. I encouraged him to start every day thanking God for his ability to work and for the job that God had provided. God used the reality of work in eternity to change Chad's perspective on work in the here and now and to help Chad see that God was with him in his struggle.

Samantha came to me for help to deal with her shock and sadness over Ethan walking away, but over the course of our time together, she began to see how work dominated every aspect of her life, and she began to wonder why. In a conversation with me about the role that work played in her life, Samantha said, "I was asking work to fill a void in my life, but it never did. I thought maybe if I worked for a different firm, got that next promotion, or grabbed that next raise, I would be satisfied, but it never happened." Then I did something that surprised her. I didn't talk to her about being a workaholic. Instead, I read to her what is said about life as people on the other side of eternity look back and celebrate. I helped Samantha face the fact that what she was attempting to do would never work. She would never find the deep satisfaction of heart that she craved in her career. Samantha began to confess that her job had become her replacement messiah, and together we worked to bring more balance to her life. Eternity gave Samantha eyes to see what she had been so blind to for years and to see the grace that she had been given to put work in its proper place.

Forever really does have the power to rescue us from both sides of the work struggle—disappointment and addiction. Eternity calls us away from seeing work as a curse and an addiction. Forever reminds us that work is part of God's eternal plan for us but that it was not designed to deliver the satisfaction of heart that only God can. Forever reminds us that our lives don't work according to our plan and that work is an essential part of God's wise plan. But there is more: forever announces that there is grace for us in our struggle with work, whatever it may be. Forever not only promises us the grace of freedom from our struggle with work in eternity, but all the grace we need to work today as God intends.

Chapter Twelve

FOREVER AND YOUR GOD

It haunted him, but he didn't know what to do about it. Casey wasn't comfortable with what he was thinking and feeling, but it *was* what he was thinking and feeling. The thoughts weren't new. They had been with him in flashes for years. But now these thoughts stalked him. He was tired of the inner battle, but he couldn't admit to anyone that this was what he spent his time thinking about.

Casey remembered well the rest he felt after he first came to faith in Christ. For the first time, his world seemed to be in order. There was a God! He was good! His Word was true! His promises were reliable! He was worthy of trust! All of it seemed too good be true, but it was true, and the hope of it all got Casey up in the morning.

Life hadn't been easy for Casey. His father's anger, the long breakup of his family, his father's disappearance, and his mother's depression that followed had left Casey both fearful and cynical. Although his schooling took six years, he worked himself through college and landed a good job. There Casey met Mark, who shared with him the message of a God of grace. Casey had never attended church, except for weddings and funerals, so he wasn't about to accept the message just because he had met a born-again fanatic. But Casey recognized that there was something different and genuine about Mark. The more he listened to his friend, the more Mark made sense. One Sunday morning, Casey went to church with Mark. He expected to be either horribly uncomfortable or terminally bored, but he was neither. He sensed an air of expectancy in the room, the worship seemed to be heartfelt, and the preacher talked in plain English and made sense.

It wasn't long before Casey came to faith. He was excited that his life had turned a major corner. He was happy to leave the pain and dysfunction behind him. He was excited about God's promises and the "good life" that was in front of him. God's love and acceptance were realities that gave hope to Casey as he had never had before. He felt blessed and was ready to share the blessing with others.

Meeting and marrying Jenna seemed like the icing on the cake. The birth of their daughter seemed to continue a life of blessing. Casey loved his wife, loved his job, and loved his church. He would often look at Jenna as he was having his quick cup of morning coffee and say, "God is good!" The "good life" he was leading became not only Casey's definition of grace, but even more importantly, his way of thinking about who God is and what he does for his children.

The morning Jenna told Casey she was pregnant again seemed a continuation of the life of blessing that Casey felt so grateful for. But gratitude turned to concern when Jenna called him and told him that she was having severe cramps and was heading for the hospital. Casey was shocked when he arrived at the hospital and was told that Jenna was in intensive care and the baby had not survived the physical trauma she was going through. The next three weeks were a bit scary. Jenna was going to be okay, but she would never be able to give birth again. Both Casey and Jenna were devastated. It was the first crack in their celebration of the "good life."

Jenna and Casey decided to be content with their wonderful marriage and their little family and to thank God for giving them more than many people ever had. Then they hit another major bump in the road. The company Casey worked for was suddenly bought out by a large conglomerate, and Casey was one of the consolidation casualties. Driving home the day that he got the news, Casey tried to rehearse what he would say to Jenna, but there was no way to make this news palatable. They had little in savings, so they needed Casey's job to meet their obligations.

Casey was angry, but he wouldn't admit it. He felt that his life was unraveling and there was nothing he could do about it. As the months of endless job interviews and seemingly endless unemployment dragged on and the financial burdens got more and more unbearable, Casey became increasingly discouraged. On top of that, things weren't good between him and Jenna. The pressures were getting to both of them, and the tension of life became tension between them. Casey woke up every morning thinking that would be the day they received the foreclosure notice, and if they did, there would be no easy way out.

It was on the way home from another useless interview, as he was sitting in traffic, that Casey first thought, *Where is God in all of this? What in the world is he doing?* The thought bothered him. He wanted to hold on to a firm belief that God is good, but none of this seemed good. He determined that he wouldn't let Jenna know what he was thinking; she was already discouraged enough. But one day it all came blurting out. Jenna was asking Casey what he was going to do next, and he said, "I don't have a clue what to do, and I don't know what God is doing either. I thought he was good, but what's good about this? Look at this mess, Jenna. Does this seem good to you?" And he stormed out of the room.

Jenna was stunned, but she was thinking the same thing. Over these difficult months, their restful faith in God had morphed into a restless doubt of God. Hope in God had dissolved into fear of what he would do next. Fellowship with other people had become jealousy of the good things they enjoyed. The joy of Sunday morning worship had changed to a ritual of duty and habit. Casey felt that he had experienced the ultimate bait and switch. He was confused, angry, and tired. And in his heart, he knew that he no longer understood the God who had once given him rest.

FOREVER AND GOD'S AGENDA

The life of faith in God is confusing. We all are surprised by what God brings our way. There are thousands of Caseys out there, people carrying deep questions and doubts in their hearts about God and his goodness. Many of these people still call themselves believers, but the life has been sucked out of their faith. Beneath the hymns and the spiritual platitudes, they feel a bit ripped off and wonder what the promises of God mean after all. They sit in the pew next to you. They attend your small group. They may even teach your child's Sunday school class. Or they could be you. Few are bold enough to verbalize their doubts. But underneath the external habits of Christianity, they're hurt and cynical. Most hide beneath terminally casual relationships quite happy in the reality that no one knows them or has a window into their true thoughts and feelings.

The messy confusion of faith is powerfully depicted for us in the shocking honesty of the Psalms. In the Psalms, life with God isn't portrayed as living in this hygienic spiritual bubble, free from the pollutants of trouble and disappointment. Instead, the psalmists cry out, "Why? Where?" and "How long?" at times when they feel forsaken (Psalms 13, 22). Sometimes they express confusion because it seems as if God is blessing the bad guys and ignoring the good guys (Psalm 73). At still other times, their vibrant life of joyful faith seems to be a relic of the distant past (Psalm 42). These psalms serve as a warning and a welcome. They warn from giving way to a doubt of God that would cause us to run away from him, while they welcome us to be honest about the doubt that wrestles with faith in our hearts.

But the Bible does much more than comfort us with the reality that we are not alone in our struggle. It unfolds for us God's agenda by letting us read the last chapter of God's story while we are still living in the middle of the plot. I don't know how many movies or novels I have seen or read that made sense only when I saw the last sequence or read the last chapter. I have watched the movie again or reread the book, only to notice things that I didn't notice the first time through and to understand things that had confused me. The portrait of forever in the last chapter of the Bible clears up our confusion and alleviates our doubt. Only through the lens of eternity does the work of God become clear and wonderfully comforting. Casey and Jenna didn't need a new religion; they needed to look at God and life through the lens of forever.

ASKING THE BIG QUESTIONS

The bulk of the big foundational questions of the human condition are not asked in the philosophy, psychology, or theology classes at the local university. For every time these questions are entertained in the classroom, they are asked ten thousand times in everyday life by moms and dads, workers and bosses, relatives and friends, the educated and not-so-educated, the very young and the very old, and everyone in between. They are asked over the dinner table, behind the steering wheel, at the wedding or funeral, in the workplace, in the bedroom, and over meals at the local diner. The big questions aren't the questions of philosophy or religion; they are the questions of every person who has been made in God's image and been blessed with rationality. We all want to understand, so we dig through the mound of our past existence, trying to make sense of the mysteries of our lives. We all are interpreters trying our best to make sense out of our lives. The way we answer these questions is more important than we may think. The answers we give will determine the way we make decisions and ultimately the direction of our lives.

Every person of faith wonders what God is doing and struggles to know how to react to the events of his or her life. Let's consider how the lens of the last chapter of life (the book of Revelation, which ends the Bible) explains all the chapters of life (which we live in the middle of) that precede it.

GOD'S SINGLE ZEAL

The single focused zeal of the Trinity is captured in song by the twenty-four elders who bow down before the Lamb, Jesus Christ. This scene of worship before God's throne is recorded in Revelation 5:9–10.

And they sang a new song, saying:

"You are worthy to take the scroll
  and to open its seals,
because you were slain,
  and with your blood you purchased for God
  persons from every tribe and language and people and nation.
You have made them to be a kingdom and priests to serve our
  God,
  and they will reign on the earth."

Imagine all that could be celebrated at the end of time: so many blessings to be recounted, so many battles fought and won, so many momentous historical moments, so many people who lived faithfully through the mystery of God's plan. Yet the singers focus on one thing: redemption. It is the subject of all the celebratory songs of eternity. This single theme accurately captures the single zeal of God for the world he made and the people he made in his likeness.

All of history marches toward two moments. The first is the sacrifice of Jesus on the cross of Calvary. The price of sin had to be paid, so God sent his Son to be the final sacrificial Lamb to bear our punishment and to purchase our acceptance, our righteousness, and our ultimate deliverance. The second event is the final defeat of sin and the welcome of all who believe into their eternal home free of sin, sorrow, suffering, and death. The single focus of God's zeal is to rescue you from sin and to transform you into the likeness of his Son.

God's plan for our salvation is radical and humbling. His agenda is radical because it is so different from the way we think about life. We want to be happy. We want to be comfortable. We want life to be ordered and predictable. We want people to like us and life to be relatively obstacle-free. We don't want to have to deal with little difficulties or major suffering. We don't want to deal with major disappointments or loss. We want lives filled with accomplishments and affluence. And if we have to die physically, it would be nice if we didn't have to suffer as we pass from this world to the next.

I think that many of us don't care about redemption as much as we think we do. Yes, we know we have a sin problem, but in our heart of hearts, we just want life to work, and when it doesn't, it isn't too long before we are beginning to harbor questions about God's goodness, faithfulness, and love. We are easily irritated with the minor hassles of life and become cynical and angry when we have to face major difficulties. Relational and physical suffering soon become spiritual suffering, because the difficulties we face force us to ask questions about God. The problem isn't that God is unfaithful to his promises or is not near or active. The problem is that we are simply not on the same page as God. What is valuable to him isn't as valuable to us as it should be, and what is valuable to us isn't a high priority on God's agenda.

Many people who profess to believe in God do not actually trust the God of the Bible. Their god is a god of their own invention or of a materialistic, human-centered distortion of the biblical message. Their problem is not only that they misunderstand what God is doing, but also that they don't understand who they are.

This is where God's agenda is very humbling. I would like to think that I am basically okay, that I am not a person in need of major help. I would like to think that I am one of the good guys, that I am basically righteous. Okay, I'm not perfect. Maybe I do need some minor tweaking, but that's all. But the truth is, I am not okay. I have a deep and abiding sin problem that I have no ability whatsoever to solve. I give empirical evidence every day that this dark thing lives inside me. Maybe I show it as a moment of irritation or selfishness. Maybe it's revealed in unkind words or a vengeful action. Maybe it's shown in an unwillingness to serve or a refusal to give. Maybe it's shown in impatience with other people or anger at my circumstances. Perhaps it's revealed in demanding to be right or in control. Somehow every day I prove I am a person in need of help—and so do you. God is working and will continue to work to solve our biggest problem and to meet our biggest need. And he will be faithful to his agenda until forever is our final home.

GOD'S PATIENCE

Already the perspective of eternity begins to lift the clouds of our confusion, but there is more. The words of the song of the elders in Revelation 5 depict a God who is amazingly patient. Again, most of us don't like to wait, but our God, in grace, is willing to wait. We want life to be a series of completed events; God is willing to live with incompletion until his work is finally done. We want what we want, and we want it now; God is willing to invest now in things that will be enjoyed only in the future. To be in tune with who God is and what he is doing means having to wait, and having to wait reminds you that you are not in charge.

When I read through the Bible, I am amazed at the generations of time between the fall of Adam and Eve into sin and the coming of Jesus to earth to provide redemption. If I had been in charge, Adam and Eve would have sinned in the morning; then Jesus would have come that afternoon, suffered and died that evening, and rose from the dead the next morning. Thankfully,

God is not as impatient as I am. The Bible says Jesus came at just the right moment (Romans 5:6). There were no wasted years in between the fall and Jesus' coming. There were no useless situations, locations, or movements of history. With patience, God was doing step by step what would result in our rescue and transformation. He never took a break. He never slacked off. He never got things mixed up. He never got tired or bored and chilled out for a while. No, in all those confusing moments of history that the Old Testament records, God was on task, moving the world toward the birth of the Savior, Jesus. We have hope for today and tomorrow because God was and is willing to be patient.

As God's children we are called to patience as well. God will not work according to our schedule. He will not always treat as urgent the things we think are urgent. Although he never rests, he works with slow and patient grace to remake us into the likeness of his Son. And he is willing to take the time that is needed to finally deliver us from our deepest, darkest dilemma: sin.

And how does God transform us? Well, he has chosen to keep us for a while in this terribly broken world, where he patiently uses surprise, hardship, disappointment, and trial to prepare us for the perfection that is to come. You could argue that the universal experience of people this side of forever is suffering. God doesn't allow us to be exposed to and personally experience these things because he doesn't care for us, but precisely because he does. With patient grace, he employs the hardships of life in this fallen world as his tools of redemption. He knows how self-righteous and self-reliant we can be. He knows how strong our trust is in our own wisdom and strength. He knows we think we're okay and the other guy is in need of redemption. So he leads us into situations that take us way beyond the limits of our own strength and wisdom. He uses difficulty to expose our weaknesses of character, wisdom, desire, thought, word, and action. And he does all of this so that we will admit our need, cry out for his help, and receive his transforming grace.

The difficulties we face are not a sign of God's weakness or unfaithfulness. Rather, they are tools of patient grace in the hands of a zealous Redeemer. He is willing to be patient, and his patient grace results in our eternal good.

As I read the New Testament Gospels, I am amazed at Jesus' patience. Often the disciples missed the point. Often they were in the way of, rather than part of, what Jesus was doing. Often they responded to him out of self-righteousness or self-interest. Yet Jesus never seemed irritated or discouraged with them. He never responded in the anger of impatience. As he was getting ready to leave them, he knew that they were unfinished, but he didn't give up on them. Instead, he told them that there were many more things they needed to learn, but they wouldn't be able to handle them right then. So he promised to send another Teacher so that they would continue to grow in knowledge and character.

I am aware that apart from God's patience with me, I would not be writing this book. There was a time in my life when I was full of myself, convinced of my wisdom, and proud of my righteousness. Because I was proud, I was also controlling and angry. I was in the process of destroying my life and ministry and didn't know it. But God didn't turn his back on me in disgust. He patiently worked to open my eyes and put grief in my heart. No, I wasn't zapped by lightning, but in a step-by-step process of grace, God undid me and remade me. Thankfully, that process of patient grace goes on.

UNEXPECTED GRACE

Because we're not on the same page as God, because we don't understand the long process of personal rescue and transformation that will finally culminate in eternity, we get surprised by God's grace. You see, because our focus is on the moment and not on God's eternal process, what we hope and long for is grace that will relieve the pressures of the moment. This means that at the very moment when we are crying out for grace, we are getting grace, but we don't recognize the grace we are being given because it is not the grace we anticipated. Because we are more focused on personal ease than personal transformation (which is God's eternal purpose), we hope for the grace of release. And we do get that in pieces right now, but what we actually need and what God is zealously committed to is the grace of transformation.

So at the moment when we are wondering why God isn't blessing us with the grace he promised us, we are actually receiving it—but it is the uncomfortable grace of difficulty that is God's tool of rescue and transformation. On this side of eternity, God's grace often comes to us in unexpected and uncomfortable forms. The grace of relief and release are coming. In eternity we will no longer experience the trials, testing, difficulties, and suffering that God employs on this side of forever to complete his work in us. Since in eternity we will be all that God saved us to be, we will no longer need the operation of uncomfortable grace in our lives. But on this side of eternity, since none of us are yet grace graduates, we still need the uncomfortable grace of personal rescue and transformation.

When we look from the vantage point of eternity at what God is zealous about and committed to, what we have experienced from the hand of God begins to make sense. He is not committed to making our days comfortable, easy, orderly, and predictable, because he is more committed to our eternal good than he is to our present ease. So in careful wisdom and faithful love, God leads us in places we wouldn't have chosen to go. He will write for us a story we wouldn't have written for ourselves. He will require us to deal with things we would have wanted to avoid. He does this not because he has turned his back on us, but because he has turned his face toward us. He has invaded our lives with patient, transforming grace, and he will use the difficulties of life in this broken world as tools of grace until his grace has finished its work and forever is our final home.

Forever

Casey was a recipient of God's unexpected grace. Like me, he didn't know he was headed for trouble. He was putting his hope in all the wrong things. In ways that Casey didn't understand, the God of patient grace was being progressively replaced by the temporary possessions, situations, and relationships of this broken world. Casey was becoming more and more addicted to the "good life," and in the process, he was becoming more dissatisfied and demanding. The things Casey looked to for life couldn't give him life. This lead to more and more frustration on his part and more drivenness to make sure that life would never pass him by. What looked like the good life to Casey wasn't the good life, and what looked like a disaster was really a tool of grace. The hardships Casey faced weren't signs of God's absence, rejection, or punishment. They were the tools God was using to rescue Casey from himself. The end of the good life was, in fact, a welcome to real life, life at its fullest, life everlasting. God wasn't distancing himself from Casey. In patient grace, he was wrapping arms of love around him.

As Casey began to understand the grace he was being given, he didn't quit feeling the pain of disappointment and loss, but his sorrow was mixed with joy. This joy was different from the temporary buzz that came from getting something he wanted. This joy was the sturdy joy of knowing he was being loved and protected by the one who created and rules the universe. This joy gave Casey strength to endure when life around him was hard. God's long-suffering process had begun to transform him into a patient and thankful man.

WEIGHING YOUR EXPERIENCE

How do you weigh your experience? Is eternity your scale? If you only weigh your experiences on the scale of this present moment, maybe you wonder if following God is worth it. You place your difficulties, disappointments, obstacles, and moments of suffering on the scale of this moment, and maybe you wonder, *Has it been worth it? Did I obey for all these years for my life to be like this? I thought God loved me. I thought he was near me. I thought he would supply my needs. I thought he was committed to bringing good things into my life.* You are haunted by these questions because you have placed your experiences on the wrong scale. You cannot properly weigh your experiences on the scale of the here and now. If you do that, you will always end up questioning the goodness and faithfulness of God.

Using the scale of eternity is the only proper way to weigh our experiences. Only then do we get a valid sense of their significance. Listen to the apostle Paul, a man who suffered much, as he places his experiences on the scale of eternity:

> I consider that our present sufferings are not worth comparing with the glory that will be revealed in us. For the creation waits in eager expectation for the children of God to be revealed. For the creation was subjected to frustration, not by its own choice, but by the will of the one who subjected it, in hope that the creation itself will be liberated from its bondage to decay and brought into the freedom and glory of the children of God. (Romans 8:18–21)

Paul looks back on his hard life, weighs his experiences on the scale of eternity, and says, "It has been worth it." Paul is essentially saying, "I get what God has been working on. God has been preparing me for something that is infinitely more glorious than anything I lost in the process. I know a day is coming when I will look back on what seemed to be crushing disappointments, and I will see them as slight momentary afflictions. So I won't lose heart, even though I face hard things, because eternity teaches me that one day I will be thankful for all God brought me through and all he did in me and for me in the process."

Have you lost heart? Are you disappointed with God? Do you think he has failed to fulfill his promises in your life? Could it be that you are not on God's agenda page? Could it be that God has not turned his back on you, but in wisdom is giving you something much better than you want?

May forever give all of us eyes to see and hearts to understand. May we look at difficulty and see God's grace. When we are asked to wait, may we remember that we are being blessed with God's patient love. When our plan fails, may we remember that we are being graced with a much better plan. And when our suffering seems too much to bear, may we remember that a day is coming when we will look back and think that our sufferings were small in comparison to the glories that are ours to enjoy forever.

Chapter Thirteen

MY FOREVER STORY

I knew God, but I didn't understand his plan. I believed in forever, but eternity had little meaning for me in the here and now. I had been raised in a family of faith and exposed to the biblical story very early in my life. I guess I could say that in some way I always believed in God and to some degree embraced the truths of Christianity. I was a compliant child who seemed to do all the right things. I was involved with all the requisite church activities that were available for my age group. I neither rebelled against my parents nor the faith that I had been taught. Nevertheless, there were signs that something was wrong with my faith.

By age sixteen, I was a very sick young man, diagnosed with a bleeding ulcer. I'll never forget my doctor, who was a Christian, saying to me, "Paul, I can give you medication that will make you feel better, but if you don't start trusting God, you are going to die very young."

He scared me, but I didn't know what he meant. I thought I trusted God, and I didn't know how to trust him more. I thought I believed the Bible, and I didn't know how to believe it more. I thought I was keeping all of God's rules, and I didn't know how to keep them better. I thought I was pretty good at resisting the temptations around me, and I didn't know how to resist them more successfully. My doctor was trying to help me, but his words frustrated and discouraged me. I did get better physically, but the problems with my faith did not heal as quickly as the ulcer did.

I ended up at a Christian college, because that is where my parents wanted me to go. I agreed to stay for a couple years and ended up graduating. There were many good things about that experience, but the worry and anxiety that had made me sick in high school were still with me. I had no problem with the theology I was studying. I had no problem believing that my life didn't belong to me. I never went through an intellectual crisis of faith, but something wasn't working. I knew I shouldn't worry in the way I did. I knew I shouldn't care so much about the opinions of others as I did. I knew I should trust God more. But I didn't know what to do to get myself to that point.

Near the end of my time in college, I began to experience a transformation. For reasons I am not sure I can explain, other than to point to God's love, I began to see the Bible as a whole instead of an assemblage of pieces. I think I had approached the Bible all my life as if it were arranged topically like an encyclopedia of religious thought or a dictionary of human problems and divine solutions. I began to see the Bible as a single piece, one great story with one glorious character at the center of its plot. I saw this story, with God's explanatory notes, in a way that I had never seen it before. I wanted to understand this story because I thought that if I could understand this huge story, maybe I would understand the little story of my life.

As I went on further in my education, I realized that I was already in this story. The more I studied God's story, the more things in my life began to make sense in a way they never had before. Right in the middle of all of these changes in my life was this thing called eternity.

You see, eternity had always been an element of my theology, but I hadn't seen it as the necessary end to God's story and thus, the wonderful end to mine as well. Sure, I knew forever was where I was headed, but I had not been taught that I needed to live with eyes on forever in the here and now. Doors of understanding were opening up for me, but I had a long way to go, and in the busyness of life, I quickly forgot the lessons God had begun to teach me about his forever story.

Between our junior and senior years of college, Luella and I got married. We had dated for three years, so we knew one another quite well. We didn't have the shock of all kinds of new discoveries that make the first few years of marriage tumultuous for some, but I carried something powerful into marriage that neither of us saw: I was an angry man. I didn't know I was an angry man and certainly never would have described myself with terminology that connoted anger. I had to be in control; I had to be right; I had to be affirmed. I had to set the schedule and get my way when decisions were made. When I didn't get these things, I would move quickly from low-level irritation and impatience to explosive anger. Luella confronted me again and again with my anger and the failure to love her that resulted, but I would not listen. I would activate my inner lawyer and tell her what a great husband she had. I would list all the ways that I was wonderful, and I believed everything that was on my list. I thought I had married a discontent woman, and I told her that repeatedly.

I was in the process of destroying one of the most wonderful gifts God had given me: my marriage — and with it, my ministry as well. But I was blind. I would ask Luella's forgiveness when, in anger, I did and said things that were wrong, but I always thought these moments were Luella's fault. *She won't listen; she always has to disagree; she is always late*, I told myself. The reality was that I was the problem, and I wasn't getting any better. As children came along, I experienced an even greater loss of control. Our first son was a tough and demanding baby, and although I never lashed out at him in unbridled anger, I harbored resentment against him for the chaos he brought into our family.

By means of rescuing and transforming grace, God used a pastoral training weekend with my brother, Tedd, to open my eyes to my anger. God gave sight to my blind eyes and allowed me to look back and to see. I saw myself with clarity for the first time in a long time, and what I saw broke my heart. I heard myself saying things that made me cringe. I watched myself doing things that made me sad. The night that we drove home from that conference would prove to be one of the most important nights of my life.

I entered the house quite late but determined to talk with Luella. I didn't actually want to do the talking; I wanted to do the listening. I told Luella that for the first time I was able to honestly say that I wanted to listen to all the things she had been trying to say to me for years. God used this highly emotional evening to begin a process of the radical undoing and rebuilding of my heart. It would have been hard enough if anger was all that I had to deal with, but there was more. Anger seldom hangs out by itself. Anger is seldom the root issue but is usually the symptom of something deeper. And if you don't get at what is deeper, you won't reach a lasting solution to the anger problem.

I wasn't zapped by lightning, becoming a gentle, peaceful man overnight. Change for me was a lengthy process, but I was now living with open eyes, open ears, and an open heart. I was hungry to dig beneath my anger and understand what had caused me to respond to the people and situations in my life the way I had. What I discovered was a huge gap in the middle of the gospel that I said was my hope. I understood past forgiveness, and eternity was part of my theology, but not in a way that made any difference in my present circumstances. This left me with something dangerous and powerful that I am convinced many people who call themselves Christians drag around. It exercises more power over the way we think and act than we seem to understand. I am talking about fear. Maybe it shows itself in a lifestyle of low-grade anxiety and worry. Perhaps it shows in moments when the person struggles to believe that God loves him or her and is near. Maybe it comes out in times when making a decision is difficult for fear of its consequences. For me it came out as anger.

I realized that I had dragged the thing that I struggled with as a teenager into my marriage. I was hardwired by God with an analytical mind. My mind seldom takes a rest. I am always interpreting what is going on around me. I am always trying to figure things out. I unpack what just happened and try to anticipate what will happen next. But all my analysis didn't result in peace; it resulted in fear. And so to deal with my fear, I had to be in control. I had to think that I was right. I had to hold tightly to my plan. I turned myself into the little God in the center of my universe. I was my own little prince of peace.

But it didn't work. I was not in control of people and situations. I was not always right. I could not assure myself that my plans would work as I had conceived them. So when people and situations got in my way I would feel the emotional temperature inside me change immediately. With more responsibilities came more reasons for anxiety, more attempts at control, and more responses of anger. My life was a mess, and it wasn't getting better — until that night of grace when God opened my eyes and my heart.

But God did something else. He opened his Word to me as well. In my hunger for help, the Bible began to look different to me. It became to me, in a deeper and more profound way, the story that I had discovered and forgotten years before. No longer was it simply a catalog of principles, proclamations, and commands. It became a cover-to-cover story to me, a story with a beginning and an end that never ends. I saw how the plot of God's big story defined the plot of my little story. The biblical story became *my* story, and I began to realize that if I understood and took seriously the eternity that was my guaranteed destiny as God's child, it would dramatically change how I thought about the here and now. I was the quintessential eternity amnesiac, and I had no idea. God used my anger to get my attention so he could teach me things I desperately needed to understand.

I was living as if the present were not connected to anything, and I began to understand that I was living between the "already" and the "not yet." Everything I faced every day was connected to the grand narrative of the Bible and the glorious end that it so beautifully paints. It hit me that if God guaranteed me this end, he had to be with me now. I began to understand that the only way I would be with him then is if he kept me now. The reality of forever began to tear down and rebuild my present. Eternity began to deliver my heart from fear and to empower it to live in a peace that I had never known. When I realized that the promises of forever meant guarantees for me along the way, my life began to change.

SIX FOREVER GUARANTEES FOR THE PRESENT

Here are the six conclusions about the present that God used forever to teach me.

1. *The future grace of eternity guarantees me present grace.* If God has promised that I will live with him forever, then implicit in that promise is the reality of all the grace I need to face what I will face in this fallen world until forever is my home. I don't need to fear people and situations, because grace will be supplied for what I am facing when I face it. I have always believed in the gift of God's grace, but after my eyes were opened, I had a new and life-changing appreciation of the now-ism of that grace. Today I can face life with courage, not because I am able, but because I know I will always have the grace I need to do what God has called me to do.

As I quoted earlier, when Peter wrote to suffering people, he captured this grace with these words: "By God's power [we] are being guarded through faith for a salvation ready to be revealed in the last time" (1 Peter 1:5 ESV). If you are God's child, Peter is writing this promise for you.

2. *The guaranteed end of the story secures control over my story in the present.* Understanding that I was not responsible for writing my own story nor able to do so was a relief. By grace the grand forever story had become my story. My job was not to control people and situations with the anxious hope that somehow things would work out. I came to rest in the fact that even when I don't understand my past, present, and future, my life is secure because I am held in the hollow of the hand of the one who controls all three. In the midst of the harsh realities of life in a world that does not operate as God intended, I can grab hold of the fact that my story will have a glorious end. God's control over his story is so careful and personal that the apostle Paul says, "[God] marked out their ["their" here means us] appointed times in history and the boundaries of their lands" (Acts 17:26).

3. *Final peace guarantees the presence, power, and provision of the Prince of Peace in the here and now.* I grew up in a house that had little functional peace, and I became a man with little internal peace. Like many others, I looked for peace where it could not be found (in situations, locations, and people). But peace is not something I have to wait for until forever is my home. The promise of future peace guarantees the presence of the Prince of Peace in the here and now. He could never guarantee me eternal peace if he abandoned me along the way. I came to realize that the lasting inner peace I had lacked for so long was not the result of the ease of circumstances or the love of people, but was mine because the Prince of Peace had invaded my life, and I could rest in his care even in moments when I didn't have a clue what was going on. When it comes to peace, I think many of us are searching for what we have already been given. As Jesus was leaving earth, he said to his disciples, "Peace I leave with you; my peace I give to you. I do not give to you as the world gives. Do not let your hearts be troubled and do not be afraid" (John 14:27).

4. *Eternal hope gives me reason for present hope.* I invested much of my life hoping for hope — that is always the quest of people

who don't have it. We all hope that somewhere around the corner we will have reason to work, fight, serve, love, give, obey, worship, invest, forgive, and continue. I came to learn that a guaranteed end gave me reason for hope right here, right now. In fact, hope was redefined for me. I think I had defined hope as a wish for something good in the future—like wishing for good weather for the next day because you're going on a picnic. The problem with that kind of hope is that there is no surety to it and therefore no security to be found in it. The surety of eternity redefined hope for me. Rather than being some dreamy wish for future good, hope became a confident expectation of a guaranteed result. Eternity taught me that I had reason to be hopeful—not because I knew my plans would succeed, but because I was absolutely sure that God's plan would. I stopped putting my hope in things and began to rest in God, who works all things according to his wise and loving will. The apostle Paul speaks of our hope this way in Romans 5:5: "Hope does not put us to shame, because God's love has been poured out into our hearts through the Holy Spirit, who has been given to us."

5. *God's work of change, which will culminate in an eternity where all things are new, assures me that real change is possible in the here and now.* My problem was that I had a short attention span. When I saw the need for change, I wanted to see it happen immediately, and when it didn't, I got angry and discouraged. I would then try to change what I had no power to change. As I studied the Bible more, I began to see that the redemptive story that is unfolded on the pages of the Bible *is* a change story. It is about how God sends his Son to a broken world to restore it by his grace. That work of change is a process that culminates in an event. God's work of change, with the intention of making all things new, begins in the hearts of people. He will stay on task until we have been completely re-formed into his image and his world has been completely re-created by his power. In the here and now, I am not called to sit around and wait for big changes in the future. I am welcome

to participate in God's ongoing work of change. The final re-creation of all things is but the end of the many moments of mini change that he is calling me to hope for and participate in in the here and now. Forever teaches me that change is not just a future hope but a present reality. It also teaches me patience.

Change in the here and now is seldom an event and most always a process. Paul told the Philippian believers that he prayed for them, "being confident of this, that he who began a good work in you will carry it on to completion until the day of Christ Jesus" (Philippians 1:6). God will continue to carry out the good work he has started in us until forever is our final home.

6. *The final restoration of all things guarantees me the help I need until they are restored.* In my transformation, the promise of final restoration took on new meaning for me. Sure, it had been a part of my theology, but it had never shaped my daily living. By God's grace, however, it began to. Think about what restoration means. The word and the process it pictures point to the need for outside intervention. Whether referring to an old house in desperate need of refurbishment or an injured victim who needs to regain the use of her limbs, the word assumes the need of outside help. The biblical story is a restoration story that ends with all things returned to where the Creator intended them to be. God acts, speaks, and comes because the broken world and the people who inhabit it are not able to restore themselves. The Divine Carpenter entered his broken-down house with his tools of restoration and will continue to work until all things are new. Restoration means I am not left to myself, that there is help for me. God is committed to dealing with the brokenness both outside of me and inside of me. "The Lord is my helper; I will not be afraid" (Hebrews 13:6).

These biblical conclusions, based on the surety of eternity, left me a changed man. Progressively I was freed from the burden of fear that I had dragged around with me for so long. I was also freed from what the fear produced: needing to be right and in control in order to make my world safe. By grace, I began to be kinder, gentler, and more patient. (By no means have I arrived in any of these.) I was able to look at people as people and not just as potential obstacles in my way. I began to be able to look at circumstances with expectancy and not just as soon-to-be hassles. The story of forever began to enable me to face things I didn't fully understand and over which I had no control. Not only did I face them, but I did so with peace, hope, and courage. I knew where my story was going. I knew I was not alone, that God would help me. I knew change was possible. God used all of these new recognitions to re-form me, and the process continues today.

I wrote this book with the hope that what I experienced, you will experience too.

Chapter Fourteen

THE JOY OF FOREVER, RIGHT HERE, RIGHT NOW

Joan has faced many hard things in her life. She has long been estranged from her violent father and is more of a mother to her depressed mother than her mother is to her. Joan didn't have much of an education, and although she isn't homeless, she has struggled to make ends meet her whole life. She has met one of her brothers — she visited him in prison — but she has been unable to locate her other two brothers. Joan still lives by herself in a little studio apartment not far from the church she attends in a poor part of town.

If you met Joan, she would surprise you — not just because she is warm and friendly, but because she projects a disarming, almost mysterious joy. This woman, who has had to deal with so much, seems to love life. This woman, who experienced all the things that we think would rob a person of joy, has contentment and happiness that seem out of context with what you know her story to be. Joan projects nothing of the anger, cynicism, and bitterness you would expect from a person who has lived through what she has lived through. She doesn't seem to be self-conscious or ill at ease. She doesn't act as if she is a victim. No, Joan always seems more focused on the comfort of others than her own. If you met her, you would want to be around her more. If you watched Joan and listened to her, you would want to experience the joy that she has.

FAUX JOY

Real joy, like Joan's, is something deeper than excitement at some good news or because of some scintillating experience. Sadly, most of what we call joy isn't really joy. Most of what we call joy is way too fleeting and too connected to our circumstances to be real joy.

I live in Philadelphia, and the Phillies (our major league baseball team) have won the National League East division title for the fourth year in a row. Right now this city is full of joy. Their win is in the headlines of all the papers, it's the talk on the local radio stations, and it's the subject of conversation on the streets. As powerful and intoxicating as this joy is right now, it is false joy and will evaporate quickly. The fair-weather fans will fall away first, and even the most committed fans will follow at some point. We will all quit celebrating and go back to our lives, forgetting the joy that swept all of us up for a moment. The championship T-shirt will eventually find its way to the bottom of the drawer. The newspapers that chronicled the rise to the top will get thrown away. The memories of the victory parade will no longer dominate conversation. And we'll all begin to prepare ourselves for another season.

False joy abounds in the world. We careen from thing to thing, hoping that the next thing will give us the emotional high that is mistakenly called joy. We spend more than we should chasing the temporary high that purchasing and possessing give us. Or we eat more than we should, craving the short shelf-life of the mental and physical buzz that food gives us. We entertain ourselves too much, hoping that the numbing joy of fantasy worlds will help us cope with the real world in which we live. We work too much, hoping that achievement will make us feel good about ourselves and our lives. We depend on people too much, searching for an inner sense of well-being in a relationship.

Ironically, for most the frantic search for joy anywhere we can find it has resulted in a joyless existence. The more we hunt for joy, the more elusive it seems to become; and the more elusive it is, the more we are frantic to find it. Few of us experience sturdy, long-term, life-shaping, transcendent joy. We run from one buzz to the next, hoping that situations, locations, and relationships will give us what they do not have the capacity to give. We live joyless lives because what we call joy isn't joy, and we are looking for joy where it cannot be found.

Faux joy makes you smile for a moment but leaves you empty and searching again before very long. Here are a few examples:

1. *Temporary joy.* This is the emotional high you feel when something good happens. It's the momentary good feeling you have as you drive away from your house toward your vacation site. That good feeling lasts only until the first sibling war breaks out in the back of your van. Or you feel good about your life when you are driving away from work having just received the notice of a promotion or a raise. You feel temporarily positive about life when your bills are paid and your house is in relatively good repair. You feel momentarily happy when a friend has recognized your birthday or given you an unexpected compliment.

A new possession, a new friend, a new achievement, a new location, or a new experience can provide an impermanent rush that we mistakenly call joy. Temporary joy quickly leaves us empty, so we have to go back again and again to get another hit of the thing that gives us the short-term high we are seeking. Somewhere along the way, we become joy addicts. The short-term buzz of feeling good becomes our drug of choice, and we're out on the streets looking for the next hit.

2. *Selfish joy.* There is something perversely intoxicating about inserting yourself in the center of your world. You get a buzz when

you win an argument and a high when you get someone to do something for you. You feel good when your story is the best story of the evening or when people laugh at your joke the most. A competitive spirit to be the center of attention makes us want a house that wows our friends, a car that is a marker of our success, the corner office, or the best wardrobe. All of these things give us a momentary buzz. We all tend to live for ourselves in some way (2 Corinthians 5:14–15). We have ways of making everything all about us, and when we succeed, we like our lives. We like the spotlight shining on us and people looking up to us. We like it when our wants, our needs, and our feelings are considered and indulged.

Selfish joy isn't really joy at all—it's spiritual thievery. The heart of selfish joy is a breaking of the two great commands. First, we don't love God in the way that we should, so we steal glory from him and take it as our own. We no longer live with him in view, but for the temporary glory of having the light shine on us and getting our own way. And second, as we are doing this, we don't love others as we should. In our pursuit of selfish joy, we don't consider the needs of others. We reduce the people in our lives to the means of getting what we want or obstructions in the way of what we want. Selfish joy is restless; it never leads anywhere good and will never result in the rest of heart that real joy gives.

3. *Transgressor's joy.* Sometimes a perverse pleasure comes from things wrongly gained. Perhaps you remember your childhood and how the cookie surreptitiously stolen from the cookie jar seemed to taste better than the one your mom put in your lunchbox. Sinners sometimes get a twisted high from transgressing God's boundaries. We tell ourselves that we have things under control, but we don't. We get a buzz from thinking we have beaten the system. We too often enjoy trimming the truth, enhancing the details of a story, and making ourselves look better than we actually are. We enjoy taking advantage. We cheat a little bit on

our taxes, and we take pens home from work. We do all of these things because in the twisted logic of sin, they make us happy.

But writing our own rules is never a pathway to joy. Remember that Adam and Eve stepped outside of God's boundaries in the pursuit of happiness. On the wrong side of the boundary, the heart beats rapidly and we feel alive, but what we are experiencing is not joy. Instead, we're experiencing the dangerous and temporary intoxication of self-rule.

4. *Delusional joy.* I remember sitting with a schizophrenic man in counseling years ago. His face brightened and he sat up straight, then leaned forward as he told me he was in possession of secrets about the United States government that no one else had. As he unpacked his delusional evidence and experiences, he reveled in every moment of it. I remember that it scared me to think that the unreal could be so real and so fulfilling. And it sobers me more to think that my friend is not alone. There are points where all of us deny reality. There are times when all of us work to convince ourselves that we are something we aren't and that we can do something we actually have no ability to do. And when we paint for ourselves a better reality than the one that exists or portray ourselves as better than we really are, we experience the fleeting joy of our own fantasy.

You see this delusional joy in the woman who tries to squeeze her size 9 foot into a size 7 shoe, or the man who has convinced himself he can afford a car he cannot afford, or the alcoholic who denies that his drinking is out of control. You see it in the aged athlete who tells himself he hasn't lost a step, in the argumentative child who thinks he knows more than his mom, or in the student who thinks she can get by in school without studying. It's visible in our fantasy that we can eat whatever we want and maintain our health, that we can spend what we want to and control our finances, or that we can treat others as we want and not harm our relationships. You see delusional joy in the husband who is unfaithful to his wife but believes he still loves her, in the person who squeezes himself into clothes that no longer fit in a vain attempt to deny weight gain, or in a young person who denies that his misbehavior will have consequences.

A distorted joy comes from rising to the throne of creator and creating worlds of your own making. A temporary high comes from convincing yourself that you are the exception to the rule, that you have more power and control than you actually have, and that you are better off than you really are. A feeling of perverse joy is found in convincing yourself that you are wiser than you are, that you have more character than you do, and that your life is headed in a direction it isn't.

Here is something humbling to think about: no one swindles you more than you do. No one plays games with your reality more than you do. No one deceives you better than you do. No one has told as many lies to you as you have told to yourself. No one has worked as hard and as long to get you to deny what is real and to embrace what is unreal as you have.

Recently a petty thief in our city was chased into a public library by five well-armed policemen. They had him trapped in a corner and asked him to come out with his hands up. He hesitated for a moment and then lunged at the closest officer, only to be shot on the spot. When I read of the incident, I thought, *What did he think the endgame was? What was he envisioning the outcome would be? In that split second before he lunged, what delusional things did he tell himself that would make him think he could overwhelm five officers, make his escape, and never be found again?*

The crazy buzz of delusional joy is not really joy at all; it is the dangerous fantasy of worlds that do not exist and that will never lead anywhere good.

Temporary joy, selfish joy, transgressor's joy, and delusional joy are not really joy at all. They are about making things work so that I can somehow feel good for the moment. This faux joy is neither sturdy nor lasting and will never lead to good things in my life.

REAL JOY

Real joy, however, is more fundamental than the good feelings you have when someone likes you or something good has happened to you. Real joy is more basic than the feelings you have when your current needs are met and you have resources to live on. Real joy is deeper than that thrill you get when you get a new pair of shoes, taste a beautiful meal, or drive out of the dealer's lot in your new car. Real joy is more than a temporary elevation of your emotions. In fact, you could say that real joy is fundamentally more than an emotion.

Real joy, joy that is not attached to a certain place, time, or person, needs forever. Real joy is vertical. It results from being in a personal relationship with the Creator and Ruler of the universe and from resting in his plan for the world. Real joy is rooted in a belief that what God has told you about the last chapter of the story is reliable and true. When we live with forever in view and when we look at life from the vantage point of the whole story, we will experience a joy that is so resilient, so sturdy, that it does not evaporate in the face of hardship.

Eternity reminds believers that this hard moment isn't all there is. It tells us where God is taking his people and his world. Eternity assures us that every dark thing will be defeated. Eternity celebrates the truth that God will win. Eternity shocks us with the certainty that death will someday die along with all of the pain and suffering that are attached to it. Eternity tells us that God will dry our last tears. Eternity tells us that God's children will be delivered from everything that is false, unwise, destructive, dangerous, and unholy. In the middle of the story, when life is unpredictable, confusing, and hard, we need more than a temporary emotional high; we need eternal joy. We don't need a momentary hope that in some way denies reality; we need an eternal hope that gives us peace and rest that help us to deal with the difficult realities of life in a fallen world.

Real joy is something more than the temporary elevation of your emotions, more than the brief good feeling attached to something in your situations, location, or relationships. Real joy is connected to something bigger than the moment and lasts way beyond the moment. You don't get real and lasting joy from a particular moment, but it enables you to deal with the moments of your life in a way that would be impossible without it. For real joy, you must look up and beyond rather than out and in.

Joy is an inner peace and rest, based on what you know to be true, that results in a life of thankfulness and expectancy. True joy is not just a feeling; it is a lifestyle. It is not the result of things that are happening around me, but a sturdy rest and peace that I bring to the things around me that change the way I think about and interact with them.

You see, this side of forever, we have to fight for our joy. Yes, it is God's gift to us, but we have to learn what it means to live in light of the gift we have been given. Here are some ways to do that:

1. *Guard your mind.* Since we are always talking to ourselves, we get used to hearing from us. So it is easy to be unaware of the influence of the things we say to ourselves about how we view life, feel about it, and respond to it. Along with this, we live in a fallen world and are around flawed people all the time, so we are tempted to have a joyless, complaining, negative view of life. Now, the goal here is not to deny reality, but to protect ourselves from a truncated view of reality that is better at focusing on the problems of life than at seeing the amazing gifts of grace the God of eternity has given us.

2. *Look for reasons to be joyful.* Maybe it is a sad commentary on my own heart, but I find complaining a lot easier than being thankful. Lasting, daily joy simply takes work. We have to require ourselves to look for the blessings, small and large, that are ours because we have been included in God's grand redemptive story. This is a part of what the apostle Paul means when he says he doesn't focus on what can be seen, because those things are temporary, but on what is unseen, because those things are eternal (2 Corinthians 4:18).

3. *Require yourself to remember what you have been given.* We must force ourselves not to look at ourselves only in light of the

insular moments of life. In one moment, you may feel alone, unprepared, misunderstood, or unloved. But if we are God's children, and we look at the video of our lives, our story is one of acceptance, love, grace, and provision that we never could have earned, achieved, or deserved. Our story has a glorious end, and since it does, we are guaranteed everything we will need on the journey from now until we are in our final home.

4. *Refuse to live for momentary joy.* If we allow ourselves to forget the reasons for joy that are found in the blessing we have been given, we will look for joy in places where real joy cannot be found. And because the lasting joy isn't found where we are looking, we will tend to career from thing to thing, hoping for the next buzz, no matter how short. It is only when we begin to attach our joy to things that are transcendent, eternal, and divine that we will begin to experience the steadfast joy of being children of God and a part of his forever story. We must tell ourselves we have reason for joy even when circumstances are hard and people misunderstand us. Why? God's forever story has given us identity, security, motivation, help, hope, and a future.

5. *Fight addiction to material joy.* Sex gives you momentary joy, as does chocolate, a good steak, a new outfit, a hot car, and fine wine. None of these things is evil in and of itself, but all are dangerous places to run for joy. Perhaps the reason our culture is overweight, addicted, and in debt is that we have attached our joy to the physical creation rather than to the grace of the Creator. That four-layer chocolate mousse cake will give you joy, but its buzz is temporary. It is tempting to buy, eat, and possess, not because we are physically hungry or materially lacking, but because we are looking for joy. Because the joy created by physical things is temporary, we have to go back again and again, and before long we are addicted and paying the financial and physical price. All of the temporary joys of the physical world are intended to point us to the Creator and the lasting joy that can be found in him and his eternal promises and provisions.

6. *Take your struggling heart to Jesus.* Since joy is a battle, you and I need help. It is easy to forget who we are, what we have been given, and where we are going. But we don't struggle alone. The one who has promised us a future has committed himself to protect and provide for us along the way. When you feel weak and overwhelmed, he invites you to come to him (Matthew 11:28–30).

Unwavering joy that does not melt in the face of difficulty is found only in knowing God and in resting in his plan for his world. True joy looks up to God and beyond to eternity and rests in the certainty of God's power and his plan, even though things at the moment may be confounding and hard. This is why it is important to be thankful that God has unveiled the last chapter for us and invited us to listen to the voices from the other side. When we do, we begin to realize what future joy is all about and where true joy can be found.

This joy takes us beyond our flawed definitions of the good life. It invites us to join the chorus of creation and the angels from the other side. This joy gives us reason to be thankful even when we are disappointed and life is hard. It spreads its wings beyond our assessment of and interaction with the moment. This joy gives us rest even when life is confusing and God is a bit mysterious.

True joy is rooted in a radical recognition that God is working his unstoppable, wise, and gracious plan, and that he will not relent until his will has finally been done! With the voices from the other side, true joy recognizes that God's victory is your victory. And when nothing appears to make sense, you can awake with the joy that his plan is marching on and that he will win!

WHAT IS YOUR WINDOW?

I once heard real estate magnate Donald Trump say that when you construct a building, it's all about the windows. Someone once asked him why the units in his buildings sold while other buildings remained empty. He said, "Go and look at the windows in their building and then look at mine, and you will know the answer." As it turns out, all of his new buildings have floor-to-ceiling windows. The same is true of life: it's all about the windows. Let me explain. You are looking at your life through some kind of window. Maybe it's the window of the view of life you were taught by your family. Perhaps it's the window of philosophy or psychology. Maybe it's the window of your own experience or the experience of someone who has influenced you. Perhaps it's the window of a past hardship that has structured the way you've looked at life ever since. Maybe you look at life through the right here, right now window of the present. The point is that you are looking through a window right now that shapes the way you see and respond to life. What is your window?

This book has asked you to do one thing: to stand in front of a window called forever and look at life from that perspective. To do so, you must:

- believe in God's existence and his plan
- embrace the brokenness of the world and its need of restoration
- humbly admit that your biggest problem in life lives inside you, not outside you
- learn to rely on and rest in God's forgiving and transforming grace
- believe that life is moving toward a conclusion; that forever is real and is coming

If you embrace these things, then it makes no sense to live as if today is all that you have. It makes no sense to spend your life seeking to possess and experience what will ultimately pass away. It makes no sense to put your hope in things that will never deliver. And it makes no sense to insert yourself into the center of your world, because eternity teaches that God is already there and is not about to surrender his place.

Forever

Look around. Take time to stop and think. Life really can't work and doesn't make sense without eternity. When you look back on life from eternity, you begin to understand what you desperately need and what God is doing. The result is a way of living that is different than you have ever known and a rest of heart that is more steadfast than you have ever experienced.

NOTES

CHAPTER 1. WHO STOLE FOREVER?

1. Benjamin Franklin, handwritten manuscript (1728) housed at the Library of Congress in Washington, D.C.
2. Frank McCourt, BrainyQuote.com, http://www .brainyquote.com/quotes/quotes/f/frankmccou203528.html.
3. PZ Myers, "Sunday Sacrilege: Imagine No Heaven," blog post, June 6, 2010, http://scienceblogs.com/ pharyngula/2010/06/sunday_sacrilege_imagine_no_he.php.
4. C. S. Lewis, *Mere Christianity* (San Francisco: HarperSan-Francisco, 2001), 119.
5. Ibid., 120.

CHAPTER 8. SUFFERING IS HARDER WHEN YOU HAVE NO FOREVER

1. I wrote a daily blog during the time of Nicole's accident and recovery that reveals our struggles and God's provision. To read my postings, go to http://NicoleNews.blogspot.com.

CHAPTER 9. FOREVER AND YOUR RELATIONSHIPS

1. Paul David Tripp, *What Did You Expect?* (Wheaton, Ill.: Crossway, 2010), 167–203.

A companion resource to *Forever: Why You Can't Live Without It*

Now Available on DVD or CD

Great for small groups, Sunday schools, churchwide events, or individual use!

Through stories, examples, and biblical teaching, your notion of an afterlife will be rehabilitated. The afterlife is not some vague, ethereal place in which we will someday reside; Scripture promises us it is a living, robust reality. In this DVD/CD resource, you will find Paul David Tripp's precise and practical applications to be consistently faithful to doctrine.

- This live recording of the conference is based on the content of the *Forever* book and is formatted on 3 DVDs in ten 25-minute sessions.
- The 3-DVD set includes a reproducible Leader's Guide and Discussion Guide provided on a CD Data Disk.
- An audio version of the conference is also available on 4 CDs.

Share Your Thoughts

With the Author: Your comments will be forwarded to
the author when you send them to *zauthor@zondervan.com*.

With Zondervan: Submit your review of this book
by writing to *zreview@zondervan.com*.

Free Online Resources at
www.zondervan.com

Zondervan AuthorTracker: Be notified whenever your favorite
authors publish new books, go on tour, or post an update
about what's happening in their lives at www.zondervan.com/
authortracker.

Daily Bible Verses and Devotions: Enrich your life with daily
Bible verses or devotions that help you start every morning
focused on God. Visit www.zondervan.com/newsletters.

Free Email Publications: Sign up for newsletters on Christian
living, academic resources, church ministry, fiction, children's
resources, and more. Visit www.zondervan.com/newsletters.

Zondervan Bible Search: Find and compare Bible passages in
a variety of translations at www.zondervanbiblesearch.com.

Other Benefits: Register to receive online benefits like
coupons and special offers, or to participate in research.

ZONDERVAN.com/
AUTHORTRACKER
follow your favorite authors